Great Escapes from the Tower of London

By the same author:

Ghosts of the Tower of London

Great Escapes
from the
Tower of London

G. ABBOTT
Yeoman Warder,
H.M. Tower of London

with verses by
SHELAGH ABBOTT

Heinemann : London

William Heinemann Ltd
10 Upper Grosvenor Street, London W1X 9PA

LONDON MELBOURNE TORONTO
JOHANNESBURG AUCKLAND

First published 1982
Prose text © G. Abbott, 1982
Verses © Shelagh Abbott, 1982

SBN 434 00596 7

Printed and bound in Great Britain at
The Camelot Press Ltd, Southampton.

Contents

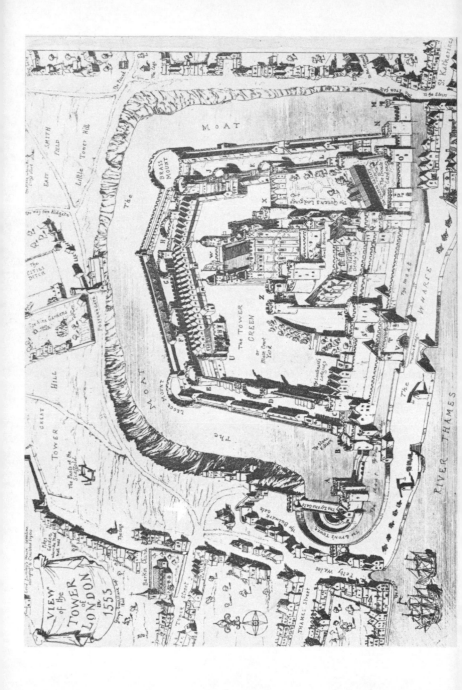

VIEW of the TOWER of LONDON in 1555

All ye who enter have a care
No hasp is snap't twixt cell and stair,
And for thy freedom's sake beware
That in the Tower thou art not trap't!

Foreword

The full title of the Tower is the Ancient Palace and Fortress of Her Majesty's Tower of London. Fortresses, which have walls, towers and a garrison have, like Colditz in our time, always made useful places of detention. There is, however, no mention of its rôle as a state prison in the title. Indeed as the dates of Yeoman Warder Abbott's exciting escape stories show, the prison rôle was only a major one for two hundred years in the Tower's nine-hundred-year history.

This was in the aftermath of the Wars of the Roses, when nobles had become accustomed to the high risks and gains of joining in the royal power struggle. The successional, religious and political problems of the Tudors were followed by those of the Stuarts, until the four Scottish earls went to the scaffold after the failure of the 1745 Rebellion.

We have no Tower dungeons, as in a professional place of mediaeval incarceration. John Holland, Duke of Exeter, one of Henry V's military leaders and later Constable, whose tomb is in the Chapel Royal of St Peter ad Vincula, is alleged to have imported that un-English device, the rack, only in the first half of the fifteenth century. The few torture instruments displayed or recorded in the Bowyer Tower show how amateurish we were in contrast with some Continental collections.

Even the axe was an inefficient instrument of execution. Queen Anne Boleyn was right in petitioning for the use of the more accurate sword.

Yet there seems to be something in human nature which drives visitors of all nationalities to demand stories of horror and to search vainly for gore in the Bloody Tower, whose earlier name of Garden Tower better suits its relatively mild history.

The origin of the Tower's sombre effect on British thinking lies surely in the daily reminder to the Saxon city of the Norman domination by the White Tower, looming to the east. What was to be feared, sometimes more than death itself, were the years of imprisonment within the high walls, often without trial and at the whim of Sovereign or Parliament.

Yeoman Warder Abbott, whose predecessors come out of history as being more human than was good for security, has rightly concentrated on the restless spark in the human spirit which drives men and women to attempt the apparently impossible. In setting out accurately, after wide research, and with imagination where history fails to record, some of the most fascinating stories of escapes, he has done the Tower a service. It can be seen as the busy village it still is, where people went courageously about their daily life, and where it was human relationships rather than stone walls which counted.

GILES MILLS, Major-General
Resident Governor
and Keeper of the Jewel House
H.M. Tower of London

Acknowledgements

Grateful acknowledgements to the Constable of Her Majesty's Tower of London, General Sir Peter Hunt GCB DSO OBE. Also to the staff of the Armouries Library in the Tower, and the staff of the British Library. Further acknowledgements are due to Yeoman Warder Brian Harrison, and also to my wife Shelagh without whose verses, research, encouragement and typewriter, these pages would have remained blank.

1. The Prison Fortress

A box of draughts is this the Tower of London.
A whistling cage of weather
Set on the city's edge.
But if you would find one chink, one slit
Through which a man may wedge his finger,
Then you have magic, sir, and there's an end of it.
For stick to stone
As skull to bone,
Tight is this prison bound.
And clever is he
Who to be free
Thinks he a path hath found.
A box of tricks is this the Tower of London.
A deluder of men's senses.
Sly thief of sanity.
What random vanity it is therefore
To thrust the blunted dagger of thine hope
Between old England's stubborn lock and door.

'When my guards told me that I was being taken to the Tower of London, I knew that I was going to be put to death.' Those words were spoken not by a sixteenth-century Jesuit priest or a traitorous earl, but by a German tourist in 1977! He went on to explain that as a young sailor in 1940 his submarine had been sunk and the crew captured. Their first prison – the Tower! And such was its fearsome reputation even in this century, even in foreign countries, that the sailors were convinced of their impending execution.

In reality, on arrival at the Tower, they were well treated and well fed before being transferred to a prisoner-of-war camp, but the ex-sailor still recalled the feeling of utter dread on hearing of their destination after capture.

For eight hundred years other men were given the same grim news, news that for many resulted in harsh imprisonment, agonizing torture and death beneath the axe.

Yet despite battlemented walls and deep moat, bolted doors and vigilant warders, a few, a very few were astute enough to seize the moment, to bend the circumstance – and escape.

What was this redoubtable castle, the first of its kind in the country, the oldest continually inhabited castle in the world? Since its construction was begun in 1078 the Tower of London has been many things. A royal residence, a royal court; an armoury and archives, a jewel house, a zoo, a royal mint – and a

State prison for the monarch's personal prisoners and other captives. Built on the orders of William the Conqueror to subdue the turbulent inhabitants of London, the Tower dominated the landscape, reminding everyone that he who held the Tower held the power. For those who rashly challenged, the prison cells waited.

During the first two hundred years the castle increased in size, its defences becoming stronger, making more and more difficult the task of escape. Early prisoners had a better chance when the great Norman Keep, the White Tower, stood alone with little more than a moat as protection. Later monarchs however saw the need for reinforcement and so encircled the central keep with an inner and an outer wall, thick and embattled, with smaller towers at intervals along their length.

The buildings themselves were of enormous strength, with walls at least eight feet thick. Everything was sacrificed to defence. To enter the castle from the landward side three drawbridges had to be crossed, a route involving a right-angled turn to deter those entering at speed and bearing a battering ram. Guards at four checkpoints had to be satisfied, at the Bulwark Gate and the Lion, Middle and Byward Towers. And even then one was only in the domestic area of the castle. Portcullises, heavy wooden drop-gates, hung in the arches, to be lowered in time of alarm. Holes adjacent to them permitted the pouring of molten lead or boiling water onto the heads of those not welcome.

A prisoner brought in through the river entrance, Traitors' Gate, would look around with sick despair. Behind him the outer wall stretched, pierced by arrow slits to repel attack across the moat, the wide ditch which, skirting the fortress, obtained its water from the river Thames and its depths of mud, slime and sewage from the primitive drains of the City outside. Before

3

him the forty-foot-high inner *ballium* (bailey) wall soared sheer to the battlements. Crosswalls joined the main walls at intervals, like spokes of a wheel, the better to bring concentrated fire to bear from above on any enemy daring enough to breach the outer wall. And through the Bloody Tower archway ahead of him loomed more high walls, more towers, denying unauthorized access to the White Tower itself. The deeper into the fortress one penetrated, the more hopeless appeared the chance of escape.

Hustled by his gaolers, the yeoman warders, he would be taken to the Lieutenant's Lodgings, the administrative headquarters and residence of the officer in command. There he would be 'booked in', interrogated if necessary and assigned a prison room.

Throughout the centuries the prison accommodation varied, depending on the rank of the prisoner, the crime and other circumstances. Some lived in comparative comfort within the Lieutenant's Lodgings (now known as the Queen's House) or, for those in other towers, furniture and carpets could be purchased and used – only to become the Lieutenant's property for resale after the execution!

The fortunate could dine with the Lieutenant, though they had to pay for the privilege. They could have their families to share their captivity, even have servants, and, if they had any private income, could supplement their rations. A certain amount of freedom within the walls was permitted; Sir Walter Raleigh for instance frequently visited friends in other towers for learned discussion, and also performed chemical experiments in a hut in the Lieutenant's garden.

The prison rooms themselves were not cells in the modern sense of the word, but were adapted guard chambers. Bars were not needed where only arrow slits admitted light and air. As many as a dozen less fortunate prisoners would occupy a room, sleeping in the alcoves, sharing the centre of the room as a communal living space. Some would be granted 'the libertie of walke on the leades over their lodginges', allowing them exercise and a tantalizing view over the London houses from the battlements. But should a prisoner show defiance or attempt to escape he would be 'close confined' behind heavy doors in the dim-lit cells deep beneath many of the towers.

The yeoman warder in charge of them generally lived with his family in the top apartment of each tower. He was responsible for their custody and well-being, such as it was.

The most ruthlessly treated however were those accused of involvement in religious upheavals or plots against the throne. Roman Catholics implicated in the Gunpowder Plot, Protestants seeking the overthrow of Mary Tudor, Jacobite rebels and Royalist conspirators; the rack and axe made no distinction. Some were 'to be brought to the torture and to be put in fear thereof, and also to the pain of same if his examiners think good'. Some suffered the final agony of the death sentence: 'That you be carried back again to the place whence you came, and from thence be drawn upon a hurdle to a place of execution where you shall be hanged up by the neck and cut down alive, your entrails cut from your body and burned in your sight, your head then to be severed from your body, and your body divided into four parts and disposed at the King's pleasure.'

Most of those prisoners lived for years in wretched surroundings with nothing but straw on the floor, little heating and meagre rations. All the towers were cold and damp. Disease was rife, and medical facilities almost non-existent. And over all prisoners of high rank hung the shadow of the axe.

But no fortress is impregnable. Defences designed by one

man can, like weapon and counter-weapon, be defeated by another man, especially if, spurred by desperation, he tackles them with audacity. Some prisoners, we know, challenged the might of authority, the awesome strength of the massive fortress, the vigilance of the guardians – and in the following pages we salute the memory of those who won through to freedom.

2. *Earl of Nithsdale: Rebel Scot*

Would ye ha'e me sneakit frae this place
Wi' neither soldier's stamp nor pace—
Bedaddled out in frills and lace?
Och, woman, find your senses.

In twenty days full twenty ways
Ha'e come to mind and faded,
And no douce wee wife
Shall save me life
In petticoats paraded.

But och, the smell o' freedom's air.
The eagle's glance, the wildcat's lair.
Enough to render soft and sair
A Scotsman's grand defences . . .

So sit awhile and tell me yet
How you and I shall slip this net.

It was late afternoon on Friday, 23 February 1716, and the sentry on duty at the Spur Guard near the Middle Tower stared up Tower Hill through the gathering gloom. At last the hammering had stopped. All day the workmen had been constructing the scaffold, nailing the planks to form the five-foot-high platform. 'They'll be adding the final touches now,' he thought idly; 'fixing the black drapes, roping off the stands, getting the sawdust ready.'

He spat into the stagnant waters of the moat behind him and shivered, not entirely with the cold chill of the evening. 'It's been a long time since they've had three executions at once. Rebel Scots or not, it's a nasty way to go — that axe is an unsteady thing to swing, and the target small . . .'

He shrugged his shoulders. In a little while he'd be relieved and could then go to the Golden Chain tavern within the Tower, and sup an ale or two.

Still mindful of his duties he eyed the people who, despite the cold and the lateness of the day, still entered and left the castle. The carts had finished rumbling and creaking in and out over the cobbles. Most of the food and kindling was delivered in the morning anyway. Now there were workmen going home into the City, prisoners' servants leaving before the Bell Tower tolling warned them. Some warders were returning from market or coffee-house to go on duty, others off out with their wives to visit friends. Not forgetting of course the relatives visiting for the last time the poor wretches who'd only see one more dawn rise above the turrets.

He watched two women who shuffled out from beneath the Byward Tower. 'These'll be two of them,' he thought, half pityingly. One, short, supported the other, a tall stout woman. Both were crying, kerchiefs pressed to their faces. The sentry half turned away in embarrassment as they brushed past him under the Middle Tower archway and vanished in the eddying crowds outside.

He yawned again. It had been a long day. Little did he realize that he had played a part, albeit a very small part, in one of the most audacious escapes from the Tower of London. But for the events that led up to it, we must go back a year or more, and travel north to Scotland.

When Queen Anne, daughter of James II, died in 1714, many Scottish lords ardently believed that she should be succeeded by yet another Stuart, James II's son by his second marriage. Clan meetings were held, plans were made; barons and earls north of the border recruited forces and raised an army. Their aim was to remove the new King George I and crown James III as Sovereign.

Finally, in October 1715, the Jacobite forces moved off and by early November had penetrated as far south as Preston in Lancashire. There, defeated by the Royal forces, the Jacobite Rebellion came to an abrupt end in disarray. Hundreds of prisoners were brought south. On 9 December seven rebel lords were escorted on horseback into London, their arms bound behind their backs. Drums played a mocking triumphal entry and the wayside crowds jeered and insulted them.

They were taken to the Tower and led each day to Westminster Hall for trial. As ever, even the most serious events have their lighter moments. Between court sessions they were allowed to lunch at the Fountain Tavern in the Strand, by permission of Colonel D'Oyley, Major of the Tower. There, guarded by twelve warders, they ate their roast beef, drank their port and filled their snuff boxes, much to the interest of the watching crowds. The Lord Chancellor was not amused. If they were hungry they were to eat at Westminster, he declared, and the Colonel was severely reprimanded.

For their traitorous acts, three Scottish Lords were sentenced to death by the headsman's axe, the execution to take place on 24 February 1716. These three, Lord Kenmure, Lord Derwentwater and the Earl of Nithsdale were taken back to the Tower of London and confined in different rooms within the Lieutenant's Lodgings. They had pleaded guilty; they were deep within the fortress; they were resigned to their fate.

But not so the wife of one of the doomed men. She was Winifred, Lady Nithsdale. Twenty-six years of age, a delicate girl with fair complexion, she had large sparkling blue eyes and glorious auburn hair. She was also very determined and very ingenious.

When the terrible news reached her at their family home at Terregles on the river Nith, Dumfriesshire, she wasted no time in tears. The situation appeared hopeless; but nothing would stop her going to London, and even appealing to the King himself for clemency.

First, however, she buried the family papers, deeds to the house and lands, in the garden, the newly turned earth quickly covered by the falling snow. The weather was appalling, heavy snow preventing the lumbering coaches from travelling on the primitive roads of the time. Undaunted, she hired three horses for herself, her maid Evans and a faithful groom, though neither woman was used to riding. They set off that same night, tracking across country and, resting only when exhaustion demanded, reached Newcastle. There fortune rewarded them, for a coach was just leaving for the South. Thankfully they boarded it, covering the miles to York – but there, two hundred miles from London, the blizzards struck again. Three feet deep, the wheels stuck fast, and the whip was of no avail. All roads were blocked, all coaches snowbound.

And so Lady Nithsdale and her companions resorted once again to horseback. Onwards they struggled, at times dragging their mounts through girth-high snow drifts. At long last, weary and chilled, they reached London and made straight for sympathetic friends. The news was black. To deter other plotters, examples must be made, and so the rebel Scots must die.

But Lady Nithsdale refused to accept the finality. She would seek audience with the King, would beg him for mercy.

Accordingly she attended St James's Palace. Dressed in mourning, she stationed herself where she knew the King would pass along the corridor. When he appeared she threw herself at his feet, beseeching him in French, for he spoke little or no English. Angrily he strode on, brushing her to one side. She attempted to push her petition into his pocket. It fell to the floor and the Countess, seizing the King's coat-tails, was dragged weeping and dishevelled behind him. The royal attendants, known as Blue Ribands, aghast at such a breach of court etiquette, rushed forward, one of them loosing her hold and assisting her to her feet.

And then the King was gone. With him went all her hopes – all but one!

Time was running short. Having failed with the improbable, only the impossible was left – she would have to contrive her husband's escape! Already a plan was running through her

Council Chamber in the Lieutenant's Lodgings, through which Lord Nithsdale disguised as a woman walked to freedom.

mind. All the little details, each preceded by the word 'if', fell into place as later she entered the Tower of London, her eyes shrewd and calculating as she measured the odds against success.

She passed through the heavily guarded Byward archway, threading her way through the domestic staff and tradesmen crowding in and out. To her left, past the Bell Tower, soared the inner wall, the high windows of the Lieutenant's Lodgings piercing its stone expanse. And at least forty feet above the ground she saw the window of her husband's cell. Wryly she thanked heaven that her plan didn't depend on *that* route!

Turning under the Bloody Tower archway, she entered the Lieutenant's Lodgings. The warders – and their wives – were, not unnaturally, sorry for this delicate-looking young wife in such grievous circumstances. Their sympathy, plus a discreet coin or two, removed any objection to her seeing her husband. Official permission could only be granted by a warrant which also stipulated that she had to stay with the prisoner until the time of the execution. That would completely ruin her plan.

Her husband's cell lay up two flights of stairs and through the Council Chamber. Guards were everywhere. Two sentries controlled the front entrance to the house, a further pair stood near the Council Chamber. A warder, armed with halberd, guarded the cell door.

She entered, greeted her husband and, wasting no time, unfolded her plan. Conventional escape was impossible, she said, and in the days preceding an execution all strangers were challenged and identified. But only all strange men – not strange women! And so he was going to walk out, dressed as a woman!

The cool audacity stunned him. It just might work. But if it didn't – ye gods, the shame of being unmasked, the jeers of the soldiers, the sneers of his captors. He'd never live it down. But to spurn the chance meant he wouldn't live at all. So he listened, marvelling at her ingenuity. And then she left him, to return to her lodgings in Drury Lane and to recruit her fellow conspirators.

They were four in number, carefully chosen. One was her trusty maid Evans, another a Miss Hilton, a tall slim woman. Lady Nithsdale's landlady, Mrs Mills, volunteered to help and being as tall and as well built as the prisoner, was more than suitable. And Mr Mills, the landlady's husband, would wait outside the Tower to conduct the escapers to a place of safety if all went well.

The success of the plan depended on three factors: to confuse the guards within the Lieutenant's Lodgings; to bluff the sentries on duty between Tower Green and the Bulwark Gate; and to exploit the belief that 'nobody ever escapes from the Tower'!

Her accomplices had to be protected from later detection, and so slim Miss Hilton became Mrs Morgan, and sturdy Mrs Mills took the name of Mrs Catherine.

It was late afternoon on Friday, 23 February, as the four women passed the bored sentry at the Middle Tower and entered the castle. The timing was deliberate, for approaching dusk would provide an additional disguise. Leaving the others outside the Lieutenant's Lodgings, Lady Nithsdale entered, her step jaunty, her eyes bright. To the cluster of pitying warders and their wives she announced that the King was having second thoughts, that her hopes were high.

In the cell she worked quickly to disguise her husband. He was to impersonate Mrs Mills, alias Mrs Catherine. *Her* hair was red and his dark, so he had to don a wig, complete with ringlets. Her eyebrows were faint, his thick; they were painted out with

14

chalky paste. His wife rouged his cheeks and twined a muffler round his chin to conceal his beard.

The door opened to admit the slim Miss Hilton, not quite so slim now, as she wore two riding cloaks. She removed the outer one and after a few minutes took her departure. Lady Nithsdale accompanied her, loudly imploring 'Mrs Morgan' to send her maid Evans in to help her prepare to go to Court, for the mercy petition was to be presented.

As they descended the stairs they met Mrs Mills coming to bid farewell to the condemned man. As only one friend at a time was allowed to visit a prisoner, Lady Nithsdale escorted her back to the cell. For the benefit of the guards, Mrs Mills was a pathetic sight. Distraught, her shoulders shook with the sobbing she endeavoured to stifle with her kerchief.

Once in the cell, Mrs Mills discarded her long hooded gown and the two women dressed the Earl in it, arranging it to conceal as much of him as possible. Then Mrs Mills donned the spare cloak left by the first visitor and, with shoulders erect, she left the room. No tears now, she stepped briskly, and Lady Nithsdale called loudly after her: 'My dear Mrs Catherine, pray go in all haste and send me my waiting maid.'

As the visitor left, Lady Nithsdale closed the door. Anxiously she checked the Earl's disguised appearance. The crucial moment was almost here. One suspicious sentry, one warder *not* confused by the slim lady, the stout lady, the pert lady and the weeping lady – and the game was up! Through the window she saw the gathering gloom as night clouds swept in over the river – the time was right!

She took a deep breath – beckoned to her husband – and opened the door!

The Council Chamber was, and still is, a large, elegant and

beautifully timbered room. As well as the guards, other people still lingered there – warders' wives, members of the staff; after all, it wasn't every day that they had condemned prisoners in the house! As the cell door opened they looked round to see what appeared to be the tall stout lady leaving, the one who had been so terribly upset when she'd arrived a little while ago. Maybe she didn't share her Ladyship's hopes of a new petition. Poor dear, she'd make herself ill, crying like that, no wonder her Ladyship had to walk behind to support her!

Lady Nithsdale did indeed walk close behind as if to steady her grief-stricken companion, though in reality to conceal his masculine stride! Her heart missed a beat as a sentry suddenly stepped forward – then she breathed again as he solicitously opened the door leading out of the Council Chamber!

Together they traversed the short passage beyond, and descended the stairs, she ever fearful of him tripping in the unaccustomed gown. To add further to the confusion she begged her companion 'For the love of God, Mrs Betty, make haste and bring my maid!' and turned back as 'Mrs Betty' reached the entrance where Evans awaited. Lady Nithsdale retraced her steps, back to the cell. Now she had to delay any possible alarm and pursuit.

Accordingly, in the prison room, she carried on an imaginary conversation, using her own voice, then mimicking her husband's deeper tones. At last, hoping against hope that they had got clear of the Bulwark Gate, she came out. With the door half open she called through the aperture that tomorrow she would bring good news, but now had to go and find the maid herself. As she spoke she pulled the string of the latch so that the door could only be opened from the inside. 'Do not disturb my Lord,' she said to the servant. 'Let the lights wait until he calls, for he is at his prayers.' And for the last time she passed through

The Lieutenant's Lodgings, now known as the Queen's House. It was through the door on the left over which a lamp is suspended that Lord Nithsdale made his escape.

the Council Chamber and out into the night, praying for the success of her plan.

Her prayers *had* been answered, but only just. Mr Mills, on seeing the Earl and Evans appear, was overcome with excitement, and almost gave the game away. Regaining his composure he helped them into a coach. As they rode away, none of them dared to look as they passed the gaunt structure of the scaffold outlined against the sky on Tower Hill!

At the home of mutual friends Lady Nithsdale rejoined her husband. For three days they took refuge, hiding in the attic of an obscure house, Mrs Mills bringing them bread and wine. They hardly dared make a sound, for the city was alive with searchers spurred on by the King's anger. Grudgingly he admitted, 'For a man in my Lord's situation it was the very best thing he could have done!' But as for Lady Nithsdale, he swore that she 'had given him more trouble than any woman in the whole of Europe'! The warders at the Tower also paid the price of being so deceived. Five of them, Thomas Davidge, Thomas Baber, Jeremiah Bird, John Cook and Adam Mason, were immediately dismissed from their posts and detained at the King's pleasure.

From the attic the fugitives' paths split up again. She, brave and resolute, took horse back to their home at Terregles. Keeping to the side roads for fear of hue and cry, she retrieved the vital family deeds before riding south again to the coast.

The Earl however had sympathetic allies in the household of the Venetian Ambassador and for six days sheltered in the Embassy. Then, in the livery of one of the footmen, he left with the Ambassador's retinue for Dover, whence they set sail for Calais. The wind, it is said, was so favourable that the captain observed: 'It could not have served better if the passengers had been flying for their lives.' Little did he guess!

18

From Calais the Earl journeyed to Rome, where the court of the Stuarts was in exile. Later his wife joined him for a joyous reunion.

Despite never being able to visit their Scottish home again, they lived happily together for a further twenty-eight years, the Earl dying in 1744. His wife survived him for another five years, and when she died her remains were brought back to this country. They now rest in the beautiful FitzAlan Chapel in the grounds of Arundel Castle.

Living as she did in an age when women were regarded as merely decorative figures who stayed in the background, may she always be remembered as the lady whose ingenuity and steady nerve outwitted the Tower of London.

3. William Seymour: Coldhearted Schemer

Lord bless the man who did the wheel invent
And placed it next its twin upon a carriage,
With an axle so to unify the marriage,
And a beast of sorts to pull it where it went.

For he did bring mobility to man
Faced with more than pack or pannier may contain,
To send him whistling down the carter's rutted lane,
And make him thusly part and parcel of my plan.

'Tis I who'll sing his rustic villanelle,
With cornstalks in my hair all thick with chaff.
And in a mild abandon should I laugh,
Should I loose the reins and give a rakish yell,
Then condemn me not on this discourtesy,
For who so is prisoner
I at least am free.

At thirty-five she was old for marriage while he was young at twenty-two. She was cousin to the King, and he was poor, ambitious and very calculating. For if James I and his issue died, she, Arabella Stuart, could succeed to the throne and he, Sir William Seymour, would be carried along with her to riches and greatness. Even without such a royal mishap, he would share her fame and her fortune. He would need to be careful though. Nearly all his kinsmen for the last hundred years had fallen to the axe. Even his great-aunt, Lady Jane Grey, had not been spared.

Arabella, 'Ladye Arbell', was an affectionate and clever girl, excelling at Latin, French and Italian. Admirers praised not only her musical skills but also her looks, for her soft blue eyes and oval face framed by dark curling hair won many a compliment.

And at Greenwich, at 4 a.m. on 9 July 1610, they were married, the ceremony being performed by the priest John Blague. James I had not been informed and his reactions to the implied threat to the throne were fast and foreseeable. Arabella was placed under surveillance at Vauxhall. Seymour was committed to the Tower.

He was confined in St Thomas' Tower, above Traitors' Gate, and there he proceeded to make himself comfortable. His name being of good repute with city tradesmen, he obtained lavish

William Seymour, Duke of Somerset

furnishings on credit: curtains, brocades, including 'Five pieces of tapestry from Jennings the upholsterer at £10 each piece', and also equipped himself with silver plate, trenchers and candlesticks from his wife's house. She, distraught, wrote frequently. He rarely replied, save to say that he was ill.

A year passed before she was able to see him again. Vauxhall lay by the river, and she managed to slip away one day, to be rowed to the Tower. There, on the wharf, she talked to him through the window of his apartment, but little went unnoticed at the Tower. Her visit, innocent as it was, caused tongues to wag. A report went to the King and within days her guardian was ordered to take her up North.

Arabella got no further than East Barnet. Illness overtook her, and there she was looked after in a cottage near Hampstead Heath. However, there was a silver lining, in more ways than one, for her aunt was the influential Countess of Shrewsbury, a woman of character and great determination. And the Countess was determined that Arabella and her husband should escape and settle on the Continent.

Accordingly the lady raised £20,000, an enormous sum in those times, to finance bribes, transport, disguises and associated expenses. Secret meetings were held to discuss the scores of details involved. Messengers were dispatched to buy horses, to hire skippers, and arrangements were made to have these and other vital contacts at their correct locations and at the correct times, for both escapes were to start from different places and had to be co-ordinated to be successful.

Between 3 and 4 p.m. on 4 June 1611, four riders left the Hampstead cottage. Two were men, William Markham and Hugh Crompton. The third was Mrs Ann Bradshawe, a female companion of the last member of the party who at first glance appeared to be a dashing young gentleman of the court. He wore French-fashioned hose and doublet, and long russet-coloured riding boots with red tops. A black plumed hat covered his wig, the flowing locks of which rested on the collar of his black cloak. The 'gentleman', debonair even to the rapier at the waistbelt, was of course Lady Arabella Stuart, and she spurred her horse exultantly, for freedom with her adored husband lay ahead.

The mounted party arrived at the first rendezvous, an inn at Blackwall, on the Thames, with time to spare. Seymour was not due until 6 p.m., when they would take a boat to Leigh. There a French ship was waiting to sail to Calais.

Arabella waited – and waited. Dusk came, and the sailors were getting impatient, for the tide was turning. By 8 p.m. she dared wait no longer and reluctantly allowed herself to be helped aboard. Safely the little party reached Leigh, to be greeted by James Corve, skipper of the French barque. He too was anxious about tides and winds, and by 4 a.m. on 5 June they were out at sea, heading east for Calais. Without Seymour, the plan was going disastrously wrong, and Arabella could only pray that her resourceful husband would hire another ship and follow hers.

William Seymour however was having troubles of his own. His escape plan was perfect, but its timing could not allow for the human factor.

For weeks he had studied the pattern of comings and goings in the Tower, and among the domestic hustle and bustle one possibility had presented itself. Almost every day, towards evening, a cart piled high with hay and firewood faggots rumbled and creaked its way under the Byward archway and along Water Lane. Opposite his apartments in St Thomas' Tower the vehicle would halt, and then the horse would be tethered to the large iron ring which still hangs against the left-hand wall of the Bloody Tower arch. The carter, a bearded man with tangled black hair, would plod under the portcullis and up on to Tower Green to deliver his wares. Turning his cart round, by Traitors' Gate, he'd then drive out the way he had come. And William Seymour, by walking across to the opposite side of the room, could watch the cart clatter along the wharf and head east towards the docks.

Being a well-behaved prisoner, Seymour had the 'liberty of the Tower'; that is, he could walk within the walls during daylight hours, and he was also allowed to have his servants visit him. So it was not difficult to talk to the carter, nor was it difficult for the carter to accept the large bribe offered to him for a few minutes' assistance. And in late May 1611 Seymour's barber, Batten, paid his usual visit, bringing the prisoner clean clothes. Hardly the usual apparel of an elegant gentleman though, as this bundle consisted of a black wig, false beard, a battered hat and a whip, all rolled up in a carter's smock!

The evening of the escape day came – but not the carter. Seymour, not daring to don his disguise until the last minute, watched impatiently as he stared through the window along Water Lane. At last, hours late, the cart appeared, the signal for Seymour to get ready. Slowly it swayed along as far as the Bloody Tower archway and then, in the gathering dusk, turned, to halt close to the wall at the west-most end of Traitors' Gate. The carter dismounted and, clambering up on to the rear of the cart, commenced to rearrange the stacked bales of hay.

On seeing this, the watching figure at the window of St Thomas' Tower over the Gate crossed to the corner of the room and down the spiral stairs which led to ground level. Here a narrow passage, its stone walls pierced by arrow slits, protected the river entrance from attack – but it also had a doorway onto Water Lane! William Seymour cautiously opened the door, to

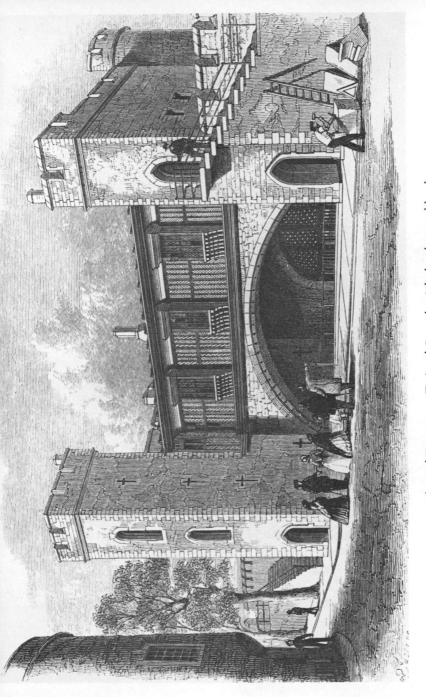

St Thomas' Tower over Traitors' Gate; the right-hand ground level doorway reportedly being William Seymour's escape route.

see in front of him the side of the cart exactly where he wanted it. The slight sound of the door alerted the carter who then dropped flat behind the hay bales, and Seymour, looking every inch the peasant, swung himself up on to the driver's seat, cracked his whip, and drove away.

Through the Byward arch they trundled, the clatter of the hooves echoing from the walls, and again as they passed the soldiers on duty at the Middle Tower. Turning left there, the horse slipping on the greasy cobbles, William Seymour drove along the wharf to the Iron Gate, where now stands Tower Bridge. Waiting at the Iron Gate, with a horse at the ready and a boat at the Steps, was his cousin, Edward Rodney.

There was no time to lose. Almost before the carter had taken over the reins, Seymour was in the boat and heading down stream, while Rodney set out on horseback for the Blackwall inn.

But Arabella had gone, and without pausing the two took a boat to Leigh, reaching that port at 9 p.m. They were getting desperate, for by now the escape must have been discovered by the warder who nightly secured his prison, and France was still a long way away. There were a few fishermen on the sea front, and so they hired a boat for twenty shillings, to take them out to a promising looking collier moored off shore. Its captain, a man named Seerson, if not impressed by the colour of Rodney's clothes, 'a full suit of satin with gold and silver lace', was certainly impressed by the colour of his money – £40, no less. So impressed that he willingly changed his destination from Newcastle to Calais, and forthwith upped anchor.

Once out at sea, however, their luck swung again. Completely dependent on the wind, they found themselves blown off course and along the coast, and so contrary were the elements that not until 8 p.m. on 8 June did they reach the Continent, and then not Calais, but Ostend.

Long before this, of course, the escape had been discovered, and the hunt was on. The Hue and Cry Proclamation stated:

> Whereas we are geven to understand that the Lady Arabella and William Seymour, second son to the Lord Beauchampe, being for divers great and heynous Offences committed, the one to our Tower of London and the other to special guard, have found the means by the wicked Practises of divers Lewd persons as Markham, Crompton, Rodney and others, to break prison and make escape, on Monday 4 June, with an intent to transport themselves into forreyne Partes. Wee do hereby and straightly charge and command all Persons whatsoever, upon their allegiance and Dutie, not only to forebear to receave, harbor or assist them in their passage anie way, as they will answer it at their Perilles; but upon the like charge and Paine to use the best meanes they can for their Apprehension, and Keeping them in safe Custody, which Wee will take as an acceptable Service. Given at Greenwich the fowerth Daie of June 1611.

One man who was not unduly unhappy at Seymour's escape was William Waad, the highly unpopular Lieutenant of the Tower. All those lovely furnishings and costly fittings in St Thomas' Tower were now, in accordance with regulations, his property, to keep or sell to other prisoners at a profit. His gloating however rapidly changed to fury, when tradesmen's bills came flooding in, for Seymour had paid nothing, and had even mutilated one £10 piece of tapestry to fit around the fireplace!

The day after the escape, the City was alive with search parties. On the wharf that morning happened to be a retired Admiral, Sir William Monson, and he chanced to overhear the gossip of the boatmen as they discussed the two young men they'd seen about the time of the escape. Galvanized at the prospect of some action, fame and perhaps reward, the Admiral hired a boat to Blackwall. Enquiries led him to the inn, and from there he reported his findings to Secretary of State Cecil.

The hunt was now switched, and while every house in Leigh was being searched, ships set out to scour the Channel. Monson himself went to Greenwich and, using his rank, ordered a naval ship, HMS *Adventurer*, to put to sea and head for Calais. A powerful craft, she made good time, and on approaching the French coast, intercepted Arabella's ship a mile from the port. James Corve had struggled with the same contrary winds that had afflicted Seymour's vessel, and now the naval craft moved in close. The Frenchman was minded to resist, but thirteen musket shots through his rigging made up his mind for him. Heaving to, he surrendered. Arabella, dejected and resigned, at least had the consolation of knowing that the man she loved had got away, and would now make every effort to be reunited with her.

Thwarted by Seymour's escape, the Law now swung into action, rounding up everyone connected with the affair. Batten, the barber, was confined in a dungeon in the White Tower, and Seymour's cousin Edward Rodney committed to the Gatehouse prison at Westminster, to which Arabella's retainer Markham was also sent. Both the latter were later questioned in the Tower of London, Markham suffering on the rack. The Countess of Shrewsbury was escorted to the Tower, as was Seymour's butler, and Haladin, a Frenchman, believed to be 'he who made the long wig for the Ladye Arbell'. Hugh Crompton finished up in the Fleete gaol, James Corve, the French skipper, in Newgate Prison, and Seerson, the other captain, was dispatched to the Gatehouse. Even Blague, the priest at the marriage, was not spared, joining the others in Gatehouse gaol.

Arabella herself was taken to the Bell Tower, the bleak cold cells forming part of the Lieutenant's Lodgings. The money found in her possession, amounting to £3000, together with the diamonds, pearls and rubies which were to have financed her new life on the Continent, were impounded. She was confined under particularly harsh conditions, given ordinary prison fare and deprived of extra servants, though later she was moved into the Lieutenant's Lodgings, to occupy a room once the prison of her grandmother, the Countess of Lennox. Lonely and depressed, her health deteriorated and, although she took the air on Elizabeth's Walk, the battlements adjoining the Bell Tower, she went into a decline. Letters to her husband went unanswered, and in March 1613 she suffered convulsions. In May that year the authorities checked the documents relating to her impounded jewels, and on the 13th of that month Sir William Waad, the tyrant Lieutenant of the Tower, was dismissed his post for embezzling some of the gems! It was also reported that a few diamonds had been legally sold to Sir Walter Raleigh, a fellow prisoner a few hundred yards away.

In July 1614 Arabella's ever-loyal servant Hugh Crompton, together with others, concocted an escape plot. This proved abortive, and again retribution followed fast. The plotters, including a gentleman usher and Palmer, a clergyman, were severely punished.

For Arabella Stuart, wretchedly unhappy, her mind far from strong, the end came on 25 September 1615, in her forty-first year. After death she was embalmed in the Tower of London by the royal surgeon, at a cost of £6.13.4, and then at dead of night her body was taken by river to Westminster Abbey. There she was buried next to the coffin of her relative, Mary Queen of

31

Scots. She had no burial service, no stone; no monument, no epitaph. So let a contemporary poet say for her

> 'Now do I thank thee, Death, and bless thy power
> That I have passed the guard, and 'scaped the Tower.'

Her fugitive husband stayed in Ostend for some time after his landing there in June 1611, but in September he moved to Paris and later to Venice. Callously he completely ignored his imprisoned wife, doubtless hoping to curry royal favour by not causing any trouble. His tactics appear to have paid off, for five months after Arabella's death, on 10 February 1616, he was granted a royal pardon, and returned to this country. On 3 November that year he was created Earl of Hertford and later married again, to Lady Frances, daughter of Robert Devereux, once the favourite, then the victim, of Queen Elizabeth. More titles were to follow, for in 1660 he became Duke of Somerset, but later that year, at the age of seventy-two, he died.

Was William Seymour really as hard-hearted and coldly calculating as he appeared? He seemed to put his own ambitions and safety before all else – yet he volunteered to sacrifice himself for his King, to take Charles the First's place on the execution block.

He deserted Arabella, leaving her to her fate in the Tower of London – yet in his will he requested that his body be buried next to hers.

But it was not to be. Within the eleventh-century village church of St Mary the Virgin, in Bedwyn Magna, Wiltshire, the searcher will find a marble monument bearing the inscription

> Here lyeth near the Body of her husband, ye most noble
> Lady Frances Devereux, daughter of Robert Earl of Essex,

and Widdow of William Duke of Somerset; who died April 24 1674 aged 74 years and six months.

Nearby stands the tomb of William's noble ancestor, Sir John Seymour, father of Queen Jane Seymour.

The saying 'in the cart', meaning that one was in trouble, derives from being placed in a cart at Tyburn, the noose tied in position around one's neck and a whip then applied to the horse.

But to Sir William Seymour, clad in carter's smock, 'in the cart' spelt freedom — and definitely saved *his* neck!

4. The Reverend George Kelly: That Notorious Raskall

Many a factor sets the heart to leap
And the blood a-surging.
Shake down a dreamer from some happy sleep
And he shall all England wake in his emerging.
Whistle the hound that silent watch doth keep,
Who needs no second urging.
Cast sudden stones unto a lake
To make the stream's diverging.
    Thus is surprise the very nub of it.
    This then the shape.
    While warding ones are yet to blub of it,
    The brazen rascal doth escape!

'Whereas George Kelly a prisoner in the Tower of London made his escape from thence yesterday, as is supposed between the hours of seven and eight in the evening; Her Majesty is graciously pleased to promise a reward of £200 to any person or persons that shall apprehend and seize or cause to be apprehended and seized the said George Kelly so that he may be secured and proceeded against according to law. Whitehall 25 October 1736.'

His description also was circulated throughout the City. 'About 5 feet 10 inches tall, of slim build with broad and flattish face, he has fair complexion, large blue eyes and good teeth.'

If the escaped prisoner could have read all that he would have felt flattered. And for his escape doubtless he thanked the Lord, for George Kelly was an Irish deacon. Born in 1688 in the County of Roscommon, he was educated at Trinity College, Dublin, in 1706 graduated as a B.A. and also became a deacon. By 1718 he was a fervent Jacobite, seeking to place a Stuart on the English throne in place of George I. Such was the force of his sermons in favour of the Pretender that prosecution was threatened, and so the same year he fled to Paris.

There he met another Jacobite churchman, Francis Atterbury, Bishop of Rochester and Dean of Westminster, and by 1720 became the Bishop's secretary. Later that year, eager to get involved in more active conspiracy, both men came to London,

Kelly taking lodgings in Little Ryder Street, near St James's. However, word had got out, and he was placed under secret surveillance. Eventually the authorities had sufficient evidence and on 21 May 1722 he was arrested. Kelly showed the spirit which was to sustain him through the years of imprisonment that lay ahead; he drew a sword and held the arresting officer at bay whilst he burnt incriminating papers – a fiery clergyman indeed! The following month he was out on bail, but was re-arrested for continued plotting. October 6th that year found him in a new home, a place from which few had departed, except via the axe, the rope or the burning pyre: the Tower of London.

They secured him in the Beauchamp Tower, in a small cell so close confined that visitors could speak to him only through a grating. There he existed for two years, and it was probably within those cold impenetrable walls that he hatched out his plan of campaign, a strategy which he would develop slowly and methodically until at the right moment he would leave the Tower far behind him.

Every prisoner under those conditions and planning escape has to consider how best to use what assets he has, whether they are his physical strength, influential friends or allies within the prison staff.

George Kelly had none of these. But he did have charm and intelligence – and immense patience. His college education had endowed him with the ability to write letters, and write letters he did, to such dignitaries as the Earl of Lincoln, Lord Townsend, even the King himself. On 1 August 1724 he complained of his harsh treatment. He was unjustly penalized, he wrote, having no privacy, a warder being with him both day and night. His five shillings a day allowance was kept by others, his health was deteriorating – in fact he had smallpox.

The cells in the Beauchamp Tower, one of them possibly the prison of George Kelly.

As happens even now, the authorities reacted in two differing ways. Within weeks his sentence was handed down 'to be kept in close and safe custody during his Majesty's pleasure and to forfeit all his lands and goods'. At the same time examining doctors advised that he should be moved to more healthy surroundings. Accordingly Kelly was allocated new quarters in a house at No. 8 Tower Green, his resident warder being Richard Madox. Not only did he have the fresh air and the outlook on to grass and trees, but he was also permitted to walk on the Parade (the Broadwalk) and even be taken for rides in an official coach, within the Tower precincts of course, and with an escort. But it was a promising start.

With guile and patience he continued to ingratiate himself with those in charge of him. Despite his indefinite sentence he seemed to have settled in contentedly, almost as a resident. Indeed it was reported on 25 May 1728 that he had much freedom within the grounds, visiting the coffee house and occasionally dining with the officers. He rarely complained, and his educated background made him popular with the residents, whom he sometimes invited to his quarters for a meal when he could afford it. He had his own apothecary, Mr Thomas Davenport, and a nurse, Elizabeth Wright. The warder, in whose house he lived, was now Thomas Holland, and George Kelly was looked after by Holland's servant maid Jane Hunt. He still took his exercise around the grounds in the amiable company of the Gentleman Gaoler, Mr Abraham Fowler.

The strategy was working well. Gain a privilege – then get them complacent; gain another privilege – quell their suspicions. Now it was time to strike again.

In January 1730 he adopted appropriate symptoms of ill health, then penned another letter. He felt sure, he complained, that if he were allowed to drive to Hampstead or somewhere similar, with an escort, of course, the change of air would benefit him. And the accompanying medical report would confirm this.

Well, the authorities thought it over, and on 6 February 1730 granted him permission, not to visit Hampstead (its air being 'too keen'), but to travel out by coach for a few hours each day, within ten miles of London, to take the air.

His boundaries were slowly being pushed further and further outwards, but limited freedom was not full freedom. He had now been prisoner for eight years, and with no fixed sentence the future stretched bleakly ahead. Having gained so much, he dared not gamble by rushing things, and so George Kelly continued his jaunts, his coffee conversations, his expeditions with his officer companion.

It was a violent attack of convulsive asthma that prompted a letter dated 4 March 1736, although an officer of the Tower described it as a 'feigned disorder'. Kelly's letter this time was addressed to the Duke of Newcastle. His last and dying wish, he said, was to be allowed five or six hours a day freedom in London. He gave his word not to escape nor to take advantage of his escort in any way.

He was not a dangerous prisoner nor even a troublesome one. He had been allowed out before, and so permission was granted. For the Major of the Tower or the Gentleman Gaoler, each of whom escorted him, such daily trips must have been a pleasurable duty. Away from the Tower, enjoying civilized conversation, the trips got longer and longer, the coach sometimes not returning until late at night. This could well be what Kelly hoped to achieve, to be out of the Tower after dark when, despite his promises, a sudden chance to escape would present itself. But either no chance occurred, or his companion was too vigilant, for despite the late homecomings, the summer of 1736 dragged by, his fourteenth year in the Tower.

And then George Kelly had a brainwave, an idea which depended on his trips into the City. On one such excursion he ordered a coat to be made, a horseman's heavy coat with wide lapels and a high collar. It was to be made of red rugg, a thick woollen cloth, and when it was finished he brought it back to the Tower. To his acquaintances however he said that it wasn't a good fit, that he really couldn't wear it, and that he would need to return it to the tailor for alteration. And he put it away in his room.

About 2 p.m. on 24 October that year he took the coat out again and, carrying it over his arm, he and Mr Fowler got into their hackney coach and rumbled off into the City. It was dark by the time they decided to head for 'home', cold too, and Kelly decided to wear his new coat for the first time. He put it on, the coach being extremely draughty, and they returned to the Tower. The vehicle creaked its way under the Middle Tower and along Water Lane as far as Traitors' Gate. There the two passengers dismounted, strolled through the Bloody Tower archway and up the steps beyond.

As they reached the top step, Kelly put the next stage of his plan into operation. Casually he said that he was spending the evening with a warder's son, a friend of his. The Gaoler nodded in agreement, suspecting nothing. He'd been in charge of Kelly for years, knew him well, and anyway they were back in the Tower now. So instead of delivering the prisoner back to No. 3 Tower Green where he was now quartered, Mr Fowler wished him good night and went off in the gloom to his own house at No. 8.

Whereupon George Kelly, in his new red coat, turned on his heel, walked down the steps, and out of the Tower!

He had done his homework well, having had years to study the routine of the garrison. From the welter of military life several facts had been carefully noted and filed away in his educated mind. First, officers of some regiments wore long red coats; so he got a long red coat of matching colour and style. Officers didn't always wear hats within the garrison, luckily, as he could hardly have ordered a military headdress. He had also observed the regularity of changes of the guard, and on this day a battalion of the 2nd Regiment of Foot Guards had arrived to take over.

As he walked out of the Tower, warders saw him and ignored him. They didn't recognize him in his coat; soldiers were milling everywhere, carrying baggage, arms and supply boxes, directed by officers new to the Tower. And the castle was in no way as well lighted as it is now; the darkness of that late October evening was hardly penetrated by the flickering torches in the iron hoops affixed to walls and archways. So without let or hindrance, challenge or alarm, George Kelly strolled out into the night.

Some days later two fishermen at Broadstairs in Kent were approached by a gentleman wishing to be taken to Calais. As the goodly sum of £5 was offered, they gladly conveyed him there, and even noted his remark that if anyone asked for George Kelly, he was safe in France. On their return they mentioned this to the local Customs Officer. However, their comments on hearing of the £200 reward they could have claimed is not recorded in any history book!

Old habits die hard, and Kelly penned two more letters. To the Duke of Newcastle he apologized for having escaped, and asked that the King be thanked for his goodness. The other letter went to the Tower of London, bequeathing all his books and effects to his friend, Mr Welsted of the Ordnance Office there. A tidy mind, had Kelly.

In France he joined James Butler, Duke of Ormond, at Avignon and, in 1744, he went into the service of Bonnie Prince Charlie, becoming one of his senior advisers. With the Prince and the Jacobite forces he landed in Scotland in June 1745. The Rebellion was defeated, though many of the rebels escaped to France. Among them was George Kelly who, in 1747, became secretary to his hero Prince Charles. He died in 1762 at the ripe old age of seventy-four.

One historian said that he was 'learned, discreet, witty, brave, and a general favourite with men and women'.

But one of the Tower Officers he hoodwinked described him as 'an old Irish Papist – a vile fellow – a notorious Raskall'.

He was probably all that – and more.

5. *Edmund Nevill: Suspected Assassin*

If I do sit thus placed
I am unfaced to those
Who peek and peer.
Alone do they behold
My shoulders twain,
My cloak that falls
In saddened sweep,
My cap . . .
And if I speak not,
But remain intent
Upon some thought,
Mayhap in time,
Some little time,
When practice hath perfected
Such raw mime,
I shall play
As if by Seneca directed
And thus deviously
The catcher shall be caught!

The scene opens in the sixteenth century, when Queen Elizabeth I ruled and Protestant England flourished. Practising Catholics were persecuted, Jesuit priests tortured and executed, with more or less the general approval of the population. Some individuals however deplored the harsh treatment meted out, and one such was William Parry, Member of Parliament for the royal borough of Queensborough in Kent.

This talented Welshman was so appalled that in 1580 he moved to the Continent and became a Roman Catholic. So intense were his beliefs that he swore his willingness to kill Queen Elizabeth. Catholic priests in France and Italy encouraged him, saying that as the Pope had excommunicated her, killing her would not be a crime.

He returned to England and sought a royal audience. Doubtless in a last attempt to persuade her to modify her treatment of the Jesuits, he revealed the plot, and in his later confession acknowledged that 'she was undaunted but I was terrified'.

His 'warning' made no difference to the severity of the Catholic persecution, and so fervent was his conversion that he decided the Queen must die. He recruited an assistant, Edmund Nevill, plotting with him and ten other mounted men to ambush and assassinate the Queen when she rode out.

Whether Nevill was an active conspirator or not is disputed. He was heir to the exiled Earl of Westmorland, and swore that

Parry had implicated him in the plot to stop him claiming the title and estate. With so much at stake Edmund Nevill moved fast and denounced Parry, perhaps in order to gain favour with the authorities. Both men were taken to the Tower of London. William Parry was tried and, pleading guilty, made a full confession. On 2 March 1585 he was executed at Old Palace Yard, Westminster.

Edmund Nevill was not brought to trial; questioned twice, he was taken back to the Tower, which was to be his prison for many years to come. Was there insufficient evidence to convict him as a conspirator? Or was he innocent, but other claimants to the Earl's estates more powerful than he? We may never know. But we do know that he was a man of remarkable tenacity. No trial, no sentence, no reprieve; just day following day, month following month, in the Tower. Forgotten by the outside world, he set about escaping.

It is reasonable to assume that, being a relatively unimportant prisoner, he had a certain amount of freedom within the fortress, and the chance to pick up bits of metal and similar useful scraps. Being skilled with tools he fashioned a rough file. Night after night, slowly and laboriously he worked at the iron bars of his prison. At last he managed to get out of his cell.

It was a moonless night. Darting between patrolling sentries he scaled the wall and lowered himself into the moat. Being a good swimmer he reached the other side – and vanished into the shadows of London's narrow, huddled streets.

His escape was not detected until the next morning, and then the hunt was on. Taverns were searched, announcements made at Paul's Cross and other public places. Armed parties scoured the squalid byways and alleys in the neighbourhood of the Tower, but Edmund Nevill had gone.

Still fit from his service with the Spanish Army in the

Netherlands, he knew how to travel fast, and by dawn was nearly six miles out of London. Passing through a village he decided to call at a shop for supplies, and there disaster struck! As he waited, another man entered, one who had left London only that morning. Seeing Nevill's muddy, crumpled clothes, he realized that here was the cause of the hubbub in the City – the escaped prisoner!

So poor Nevill was arrested and under heavy escort taken back to the Tower. As punishment he was close confined, secured by leg irons chained to a wooden pillar in his cell.

Time passed, and having caused no trouble, or had no opportunity to, he was released from his bonds. Indeed he was given a bonus, for in 1588 he applied for his wife to visit him, and in 1590, upon a change of Lieutenant of the Tower, the list of prisoners included:

'Edmonde Nevill, esquior, hath the libertie of the Tower, by warrant bearing date the xvi daie of September 1590 signed by the lord chauncellor etc. and the same warrant geveth accesse unto his wife and all his freinds.'

A privilege indeed, but only complete freedom would satisfy him. Still in possession of his file, he put it to work again. In his daily walks in the grounds, possibly he discovered that his previous escape route had been blocked, that he needed to scale a higher wall than before. Accordingly he obtained a length of rope, and one dark night he tried again.

Out of the cell he went, via shadows, to the encircling wall. He climbed up the rope to the battlements, then slid down towards the waters of the moat. To his horror he found that the rope was short, much too short! For long moments he weighed the odds, then decided to drop. Taking a deep breath, for the moat was slimy and evil smelling, he let go.

There was a loud splash, so loud that it alerted the sentries pacing within the castle. Swimming desperately he emerged from the stagnant waters just as the soldiers burst out on to the wharf. Quickwitted as ever, he turned and ran, shouting 'Stop him! There he goes!' as behind him the soldiers gave pursuit.

The leading soldier however didn't see why the fellow ahead of him should get all the glory of the recapture. Speeding his step he drew level. Then seeking to pass, he put his hand out to pull the man back and overtake him. And his hand landed on a soaking wet shoulder!

Once more he was punished, close confined to his cell. His limbs were manacled, but not his brains. Twice he had tried to escape via the moat; twice its wetness had betrayed him. Very well then, he would take a different route, at a different time – as a different person. And when he was given limited freedom once more, he had a beautifully polished plan ready to put into action.

In his cell he adopted new tactics. Every time his warder, Henrie Frewen, entered, there would be the prisoner sitting at the barred window, motionless and silent. This behaviour hardly surprised the warder. Many prisoners after recapture turned sullen and depressed, brooding over their misfortune. As the weeks went by, the warder got used to seeing the still figure against the light from the window, huddled up to keep warm, and obviously staring bleakly out over the battlemented walls. 'He must have learned his lesson,' the warder concluded. 'Pity he didn't realize sooner that you can't beat the Tower!'

But each time, as soon as the bolts slammed to in the heavy door and the warder's shuffling footsteps had died away down the spiral stairs, Nevill sprang into action, continuing his preparations. This time he would not be thwarted!

On the day planned, he was up early. First he deftly assembled a dummy figure, stuffing it with his spare clothes and

Edmund Nevill

positioning it in his habitual window seat. He bent it slightly forward and draped his usual hooded cloak around it. From the door it looked, well, just as he thought *he* looked! He pulled out from under his ramshackle bed the items he had manufactured for his disguise, and started to transform his appearance. Edmund Nevill, prisoner, was going to vanish, to be replaced by Edmund Nevill – blacksmith!

He had carved a set of tools out of wood, smearing them black for realism. Odd lengths of leather and cloth sewn together provided him with a typical smith's apron. A thonged belt completed the outfit, a belt from which he hung the various implements he had made. Rolling up his sleeves, he rubbed dirt into his arms and hands, daubing some across his cheek, then ruffled his hair, in an attempt to present a workmanlike appearance.

It was nearly time for the warder's first visit. Nevill took one last look round, then crossed to the alcove beside the door, and waited.

Soon he heard his gaoler's footsteps, heard the ponderous bolts drawn back. The door swung open, concealing him, and the warder entered the room bearing the tray of food. And as the man, without a word to the still figure in the window, advanced towards the table, Nevill rounded the door and silently sped down the stairs!

He emerged into the daylight, the glorious fresh-air feel of freedom momentarily making his senses reel. Wasting no time he moved away – but had only gone a few yards when he was suddenly assailed by a woman's voice.

'Who are you?' she queried suspiciously. 'Where are you going?'

His heart sank with dismay. 'Out!' he said gruffly. 'I've been doing a job up there!' And he jerked a grimy thumb at the low-arched doorway behind him. Her eyes narrowed.

'You're not allowed in this area without an escort – I'm going to report you!'

Even as she spoke, his warder came down the stairs, and almost unbelievingly stared at the pseudo-blacksmith.

'Not again!' he breathed in amazement. 'Come on, back to your cell!'

Some two years later, however, fortune favoured Edmund Nevill. In 1598, after thirteen years in the Tower of London, he was released. He lived peacefully on the Continent with his wife Jane and their three sons and four daughters. He still sought to establish his right to the title of Earl of Westmorland, but in this he failed, despite petitioning King James I.

In 1640, forty-two years after his release from the Tower, he died in Brussels. In the twelfth-century parish church of Saint Mary Magdalene in East Ham, London, stands a magnificent monument complete with superb effigies of the members of the family. Above them the tablet reads:

IN MEMORIA SACRUM

'In memory of the Right Honorable EDMOND NEVILL Lord Latimer, Earl of Westmorland, and Dam Jane his wife with the memorials of their seven children. Which Edmond was lineally descended from the honorable blood of Kings and princes in ye line of ye 7th Earl of Westmorland of the name of Nevill.'

A man of unquenchable spirit, he deserved his happy ending.

6. *John Gerard, Francis Arden: Fugitive Catholics*

Here a very puzzlement we have . . .
Some salt, a cradle and a lowly orange.
But no poringer is needed
For this meal,
Nor yet a child to lullay unto sleep.
For the Salt and Cradle are but Tower prisons,
And the orange doth a dual purpose keep.
For when the gentle juice
So eased his lips,
This man of faith
With broken fingertips,
Did painfully the orange peel emboss
To form his Master's symbol
Of a cross.

A double escape, this; one man imprisoned for ten years awaiting execution, the other, a priest, cruelly tortured after only six months in the Tower. How they achieved it is an object lesson in blackmail, deception and sheer human courage.

John Gerard was a Jesuit priest; like his father, Sir Thomas Gerard of Lancashire, he sought fervently to spread the aims of the Roman Catholic Church through England in an age when, under Queen Elizabeth, practising priests were hunted down and jailed or worse. Indeed John's father had twice been confined in the Tower of London for plotting to free Mary, Queen of Scots.

His son did much of his religious training on the Continent and then in 1582, at the age of eighteen, he returned to this country. For the next twelve years he moved around, performing his priestly duties in defiance of the law. Most of the time he kept one move ahead of the authorities. Other times he was arrested, imprisoned, interrogated and then released.

By 1594 he had gained the reputation, rightly, of being one of the leading Jesuits in England. By the Protestant Queen and Government he was regarded as a dangerous conspirator, a thorn in their sides. He would have to be plucked out.

In the spring of that year, despite every precaution, even concealment in priest holes behind false panelling, Gerard was captured. He was taken to the Counter prison and later to the

Clink, a gaol so infamous that its very name became a slang term for prison. For three years he was penned up and questioned, occasionally chained and always harshly treated. The man would not confess, would not reveal the web of others spread throughout the country. Not only stubborn, he even attempted to escape, using counterfeit keys. To the Tower then he must go.

And in April 1597, to the Tower he was taken. His particular prison there was the Salt Tower, a massive stone bastion at the south-east corner of the inner wall. He was placed in the charge of Bonner, a warder humane and kindly, qualities not shared by those who, within the next few days, were to put Gerard to the torture.

He was escorted to the deepest chamber in the White Tower, a vault without windows or outer doors. There, in the eerie glow of flickering torches, he was urged to confess. He refused. He was then hung up by his arms, his wrists through iron gauntlets, his feet clear of the ground, and was left for hours to endure the excruciating agony. Several times he fainted, each time he was revived – and the torture reapplied. Evening came, and Gerard was helped back to his cell, suffering but still loyal to his colleagues.

The next day the appalling torment was repeated in the morning and again in the afternoon. At last, numbed and semiconscious, he lurched back to the Salt Tower, his hands swollen monstrously, his arms and shoulders throbbing with unbearable pain. Because he was unable to move his fingers, his warder Bonner cut up some food and fed him with small pieces, the man visibly upset at the condition of his prisoner.

As the time went by, Gerard was left undisturbed in the Salt Tower, but never knowing when next he would be subjected to the gauntlets or even the rack. He passed the lonely hours in prayer and, being a practical man, in doing finger exercises, though it was three weeks before he could once more feed himself, and a further six months until he regained full sense of touch.

As another worthwhile occupation he ingratiated himself with his warder. Prisoners were allowed to contact friends outside in order to obtain clothing, bedding and suchlike, and Bonner was the link. Among other things, Gerard asked for, and obtained, some oranges and a toothpick. From the orange skin he cut out rosaries for worship. From the toothpick he made a pen. His 'ink' was the orange juice, visible only when heated, which he used for secret messages on the ordinary charcoal-written letters to outside friends.

The correspondence continued for six months. Bonner, sympathetic by nature and doubtless influenced by Gerard's strong personality, soon consented to carry sealed, uncensored letters back and forth. He also accepted money for these services, thus unwittingly placing himself in Gerard's power. No visitors were allowed, yet the warder, suitably bribed, admitted callers under the pretext of their being acquaintances of Mrs Bonner. And all the time Gerard's contacts were ready and waiting for any escape bid. The scene was set.

Thirty yards or so away from the Salt Tower stands the Cradle Tower, a much smaller building, on the outer wall. It overlooks a narrow stretch of the moat, on the other side of which, in those days, stood a high wall. Beyond the wall was the wharf and the river.

Within the Cradle Tower, Francis John Arden was imprisoned. A Catholic gentleman from Evenley, Northamptonshire, he had lain under sentence of death for the past ten years, on a charge of plotting against Queen Elizabeth. His wife frequently visited him, bringing clean clothes and food in a

The Cradle Tower from the wharf

basket. Again custom dulled suspicion; the basket was rarely if ever searched.

By signalling from his window, Gerard established contact with Arden, and by degrees manipulated warder Bonner into taking letters across, for which he paid him, of course. Later on, an even larger reward overcame Bonner's fears, and Gerard achieved a minor victory, to be allowed to visit Arden, stay overnight and celebrate Mass. Arden's wife brought in the necessary holy articles, and the two men prayed together. And because of the Cradle's proximity to freedom, they also discussed escape.

Back in the Salt Tower Gerard got down to details. Letters went in and out, arranging for ropes, a boat, outside helpers and later assistance.

But why not simply bribe the warder handsomely to let Gerard walk out suitably disguised? Well of course, they tried. One of Gerard's friends offered Bonner a thousand florins down and another hundred a year for life. But even a bribe that large would not compensate for being branded an outlaw, and hanged if caught, so Bonner refused even to consider it.

The planned evening came, and Gerard joined his friend in the Cradle Tower, Bonner locking them in. Unfortunately he'd also locked the door to the flat roof, so the two prisoners had to chip away the stonework around the bolt. Once out, they waited until midnight, when the rescue boat, manned by John Lillie and Richard Fulwood came alongside the wharf. As it did so, a resident of one of the little houses nearby came out and conversed with them. Agonizing moments passed, the man's suspicions having to be allayed, but by then it was too late – the tide had turned! The watchers on the turreted roof, bitterly disappointed, turned away, only to hear frantic shouts from their would-be rescuers, for the boat had got trapped in the fearsome millrace beneath London Bridge a few hundred yards away. There, between the piers, the current surged and swirled, a hazard dreaded by all boatmen. Ropes were lowered from the bridge, other boats put out, and against all the odds, the men were dragged to safety.

Next day the messages flowed again, fixing a new date a week or so later, for 5 October 1597. The unsuspecting Bonner permitted the visit to the Cradle Tower, and at the appointed time Gerard and Arden mounted to the roof. Hardly daring to breathe for fear of alarming the pacing sentry below and behind them, they anxiously peered out towards the approaching craft. The two who disembarked wore white cloths on the front of their jackets as identification, and so the men on the tower top went into action.

A small iron ball with cord attached was hurled out and over the moat and wall, to clatter on the cobbled wharf. One rescuer seized it and, tying strong rope to its end, gave the prearranged signal. Arden pulled, bringing cord and rope to him, then secured the rope to a cannon mounted on the roof. The men on the wharf tied their end to a convenient stake; the moment had come, and all the prisoners needed to do was to slide down on to the wharf. But one vital calculation had been overlooked. The wharf wall was nearly as high as the tower battlements, and the rope, being heavy, sagged between. Arden, struggling across first, caused it to stretch and sag even more. Gerard prayed, then grasped the rope, wincing as it bit into his numbed, mutilated hands.

Even as he moved a yard into the black space above the sullen waters of the moat, disaster struck, his body spinning round to hang beneath the rope as he locked it between his knees. Somehow he managed to inch his way along, unable to see how far he must go, yet terrifyingly aware of the slackening rope.

59

Every gasp from his panting lungs seemed to echo in the chasm of tower and wall; sentries were only yards away, and now, as he struggled past the half-way point, the rope started to slope upwards.

Surely, whatever faith one embraces, credit must be given to some force, some power which, when all strength is spent and hope is lost, emerges to re-endow a person with almost supernatural determination. So it was with John Gerard. Scrabbling with hands and legs he clawed his way to the wall. There, completely exhausted, he swung, unable to surmount the final obstacle. Pebbles fell from its parapet, to plop noisily in the moat below, and the fibres of the rope rasped against the wall's rough edge. Suddenly the rope vibrated, as John Lillie swarmed up from the other side, to grasp Gerard and, somehow, bodily haul him over the wall.

On the wharf Gerard collapsed, as well he might. One helper revived him while the others hacked the rope away, taking care not to let any of it fall and splash into the moat. Gently Gerard was lifted into the boat, strong arms wielded the long oars, and the fugitives were whisked away to a safe hiding place on the outskirts of the city.

John Gerard had arranged for three letters to be delivered, one to the Lieutenant of the Tower absolving the warder of any blame, and one to the Lords of the Council similarly exonerating the Lieutenant. The third he sent by hand to Warder Bonner, urging him to flee to Gerard's friends who would shelter him and pay him two hundred florins a year. Bonner, knowing too well the vengeance of the law, wisely and rapidly accepted. On horseback he rode north to a 'safe house' in the country. Later, joined by his family and supported by the promised annuity, he became a Catholic, and lived peacefully until his death in 1602.

Little is known of Francis John Arden following his escape, though as his name did not reappear in the Tower records, it is reasonable to assume that he was successful in evading recapture.

John Gerard, with his boundless spiritual stamina, simply continued with his work as a priest. For a while he recuperated at Kirby Hall in Northamptonshire, but then moved throughout the country as before, the pack always at his heels. The year 1605 came, bringing with it the Gunpowder Plot to blow up King and Parliament. Most of Gerard's friends and colleagues were implicated, and in the great round-up that followed, priests and plotters alike were hanged, drawn and quartered. The spies were also out for the tall swarthy man, hawk-nosed and short-bearded, who had a slight lisp and a ready smile; the hunt was on to capture John Gerard.

So intense was the search that six months later, in May 1606, Gerard slipped unobtrusively away to the Continent in the retinue of the Spanish and Dutch Ambassadors. He later moved to Rome where, at the goodly age of seventy-three, he died on 27 July 1637.

Traitor or Man of God; blackmailer or patriot; conspirator or saint; it doesn't really matter now.

But he *was* a brave man.

7. *Arthur, Lord Capel: Daring Cavalier*

It hath rained all day.
And every drip
From out the leaden sky
Hath drop't with deadly certitude
Upon this prison.
   The whole Tower weeps.
But when it sleeps,
All damply clung
Unto its ancient clay,
I shall be gone.
I shall be fled.
I shall be quite away.
For taking to myself
This elemental christening
Shall feel God-blest,
As I put faith and courage,
Might and main,
Unto the test.
   'Tis but a rope's length.
   My muscles' strength.
   And I am past all petty prisoning.

In 1648 the Civil War still dragged on. Brother fought brother, father clashed with son. Eventually Cromwell and his Roundheads gained the upper hand and Charles I surrendered his authority as King.

Various battles had raged throughout the country, many towns being besieged. One such was Colchester, where for weeks its castle defied repeated attacks by the Roundheads. At last the Royalist defenders had to capitulate and their commander, Arthur, Lord Capel, was taken under escort first to Windsor Castle, then to the Tower of London.

Lord Capel was one of Charles' most loyal supporters, so valued in fact that the King had created him first Baron of Hadham, in Hertfordshire. He had married Elizabeth, daughter and heiress to Sir Charles Morrison of Cashiobury, Wiltshire, by whom he had had five sons and four daughters. An extremely tall man, he was noted for his patriotism and devotion to his monarch.

In the Tower he was frequently visited by his friends. Many people were still secretly sympathetic to the Royalist cause, and the final outcome of the political struggle could not be foreseen.

Lord Capel decided to escape and, with the instincts of a military man, employed a method that required no finesse or subterfuge. He would wade across the moat.

His friends knew of a shallow route, perhaps formed where

the dumped refuse had piled higher, or where sluice waters had deposited sand and rubbish. Arthur Capel was a brave man and he was desperate to escape, for he knew that no mercy would be shown at his trial. He could not swim, and the Tower 'ditch' was a fearsome place; twelve to fifteen feet deep, half full of mud and slime, its stagnant waters were rarely disturbed by the tides supposedly admitted by the sluice gates. Indescribable filth from the castle and the city poured into it. Thirty yards wide in places, its far banks were not, as now, neatly bricked and vertical; a shallow muddy slope ran from the surrounding path down to the weed-covered surface, a death trap for wandering cattle or drunken revellers.

Yet Capel made the decision. His only assets were his considerable height and his undeniable nerve. Both would be tested to the full in the coming ordeal.

His friends smuggled in rope, doubtless wound around their bodies under their cloaks, and grappling irons wrapped up in bundles of extra clothing for the prisoner. The Tower was crowded with Royalist captives and it would seem that Lord Capel was in a tower not as secure as most, having a window widely barred.

The planned night came, dark and misty. He looped the rope round the bars and eased himself out on to the narrow ledge beyond. Down the rope he went, into the shadows of the outer ward, the domestic area of the castle. A few quick paces, his ears straining for the sentries' measured tread, and he was up on to the outer wall. Stealthily he worked his way along the battlements until he judged himself to be poised above the 'shallow' route he needed. Deftly he secured the grappling irons to the stonework, throwing the rope over the side. Then hand over hand he lowered himself into the blackness below.

Within seconds his feet reached the surface of the moat. Not daring to make a sudden splash, he slowly immersed himself in the evil-smelling water, its coldness sending shivers through him as it crept higher. Down he went, the water reaching his chest before his feet touched the muddy bottom. For a long moment he held on to the rope in terrible indecision. Before him, the sullen menace of the waters; behind him, the axe. He took a deep breath, released the rope – and stepped forward. And the water rose higher.

Groping with his feet he fought to maintain his balance as each step sank into soft yielding mud. The water now was up to his chin, and as his eyes were almost on a level with the surface it was impossible to see just how far away the bank was. Or indeed whether he'd unwittingly turned and was struggling round the moat rather than across it! Panic gripped him, stench filling his nostrils from the bubbles rising to the surface as his hesitant steps disturbed the ooze on the bottom. With a superhuman effort he pushed on, swaying on tip toe in order to keep nose and mouth above water level. As in a nightmare he struggled, refusing to imagine his next step encountering an even softer patch of mud, or, heaven forbid, a deep hole – when without warning his foot struck harder ground, and his chin lifted clear of the slime. He was through!

In a state of near collapse, he sprawled on the bank. Then, aware of the need for haste, he dragged himself up and on to the path. Shadowy figures approached. Too exhausted to run, Lord Capel found himself embraced by his anxious friends. They had almost given him up for lost, having waited where he should have emerged only a few yards away.

Quickly he was hustled away through the dark alleys to where a private coach awaited, and within the hour he was safe and dry in a sympathizer's house in the City. For two or three days he remained hidden there, while the hunt for him ranged

66

far and wide. So wanted was the fugitive that it was decided he should be transferred to a safer hide-out south of the river.

Accordingly, suitably muffled, he and his friends hailed a boat at Temple Steps one dark night, to be rowed across the Thames to Lambeth Marsh. It was then that Lord Capel's fortunes deserted him. Whether the boatman was suspicious or whether, as some say, he overheard one gentleman address the very tall one as 'My Lord' will never be known. But, when he had ferried them ashore up river he discreetly followed them and noted their address. Off then to an officer he went, and reported his discovery. After claiming the reward of £20 and the promise of employment with the Admiralty, he led the searchers to the hide-away. For Arthur Capel the game was up.

He was taken back to the Tower and later put on trial. His wife raised a petition on his behalf, and such was his prestige in the country that a great debate took place in Parliament. Even Cromwell praised his loyalty to the throne, adding that because of such integrity he would have to die. And die he did.

Though sentenced to be hanged, this was commuted to the more honourable one of beheading. On 9 March 1649, in New Palace Yard outside Westminster Hall, the axe descended. Ironically the dread weapon was wielded by Richard Brandon, esquire, who was thought to have been, five weeks earlier, the masked executioner of Lord Capel's monarch, King Charles I. Brandon himself died later that year, some say of remorse at killing a King.

In the graveyard of St Cecilia's Church at Little Hadham, the soft wind sighs through the trees, and the peacocks shriek. Inside the fourteenth-century church Lord Capel and his lady rest within the family vault beneath the altar. Their tomb bears the inscription:

'Hereunder lieth interred the body of Arthur, Lord Capel, Baron of Hadham, who was murdered for his loyalty to King Charles the First 9th March 1649.
Here lyeth interred ye body of Elizabeth, Lady Capel, wife of Lord Capel, onely daughter of Sir Charles Morrison Kt. She departed this life ye 26th of January 1660'

And the boatman? Oh, he had to wait until November before receiving his blood money – and doubtless felt himself unjustly treated by the delay.

The Capel tomb in St Cecilia's Church, Little Hadham, Hertfordshire

8. *John Lambert: Knight of the Golden Tulip*

As the bee feedeth on the flower
So would I take one shining hour
And crush the honey from it.
Each minute-making second
To be elaborately reckoned
As doth man with moon
Or luminary comet.

Caught as I am
Within the tendrils of some treason,
Each natural season
Leaves its mark on bark or bower,
Yet I am held.

Would I could grasp the golden trumpet
Of my homage
Strong within my hand,
And at its call
Declare man's freedom
Through the land.

If our escapers adopted the instruments of their escape as their family crest, some would include a length of rope or a blacksmith's apron, even a woman's dress. Colonel John Lambert's crest would however look rather strange, portraying a silken garter and a woollen nightcap!

Not that he was in any way unmanly. On the contrary he was a military commander of fine repute, daring and brave. At the outbreak of the Civil War in 1642 he answered the call to arms. He was then twenty-three years old and had been married for three years to Frances, daughter of Sir William Lister of Thornton-in-Craven in Yorkshire, not far from his own home at Calton.

He soon proved to be an outstanding soldier, leading his Roundhead troops into battle after battle. During the siege of Pontefract in March 1645 he was wounded, yet in the following year as commander of a regiment of foot he recaptured Appleby and four other castles. Always in the thick of the fighting, he seemed to lead a charmed life, for on 3 September 1651 his horse was shot while he was in the saddle.

Throughout the campaigns, Lambert's reputation steadily increased. In fact Cromwell told Parliament that Lambert was worthy of their note, to which they responded by granting him lands in Scotland to the value of £1000 a year. As one of the senior military commanders, he involved himself in politics, soon rivalling Cromwell for the ascendancy. Indeed one Royalist commented: 'It lies within Lambert's power to raise Cromwell higher – or to set up in his place.'

1657 was John Lambert's year. The Army's darling, he was Major-General, Colonel of two regiments, Member of the Council ruling the country and a Lord of the Cinque Ports. His income from these posts totalled £6500 per year, and such was their effect on his ambitious nature that his critics said he was 'too soon putting on the Prince', i.e. getting too big for his boots.

Evidently Cromwell thought the same. Wary of Lambert's influence and popularity with the army, later that year he retired Lambert on a pension of £2000 a year.

This must have been a shattering blow to John Lambert's dreams, yet his fierce loyalty to his principles left him no option. To compete with Oliver Cromwell could have upset the brittle state of the country, could even have opened the way for the plotting Royalists to regain power, and Lambert would never accept that.

So he retired, living peacefully in his house in Wimbledon.

In 1658 Cromwell died, to be succeeded by his son Richard, a man lacking the qualities required to rule the country. Eventually he dissolved Parliament and John Lambert, sensing the need for a strong man, re-emerged into public life. But by now the people wanted the return of the monarchy. On 13 October 1659, Lambert and his troops surrounded Westminster and prevented the Members from taking their seats in Parliament. This, and other similar scenes of turbulence, caused the Army to be disbanded. On 26 January 1660 Lambert was accused of mutiny and ordered to pay £20,000 surety to be of good behaviour. He couldn't pay, and so was committed to the Tower of London.

Here then, imprisoned in St Thomas's Tower over Traitors'

Gate, was this gifted and talented man, convinced that his destiny was to restore the country's confidence as a Commonwealth, and to crush the Royalist ambitions once and for all. Despite the odds he *had* to escape.

In order to achieve this, he needed help both inside and outside the Tower, and in this he was fortunate. His personality and reputation were well known, and among the officials in charge of the prisoners he must have had many sympathizers, for old loyalties die hard. Nevertheless no one was prepared to be openly responsible for his escape; retribution followed fast and sure on those who released their charges. But messages *could* be conveyed, and sentries told to look the other way.

Clouds covered the night sky on 11 March 1660, and a watcher on the wharf, had he been near enough, would have seen a shadowy figure ease himself through a narrow upper window of St Thomas's Tower. The exact details of Lambert's route are not recorded, but we know that a silken rope was thrown down from the window, a rope romantically described later as a 'garter made by a lady for which she received £100'.

The dark figure, hands swathed with cloth to protect them from friction, slithered down the rope and gained access to the wharf where, by timing or arrangement, he evaded the patrolling sentries. Oars manned by twelve strong arms splashed briefly at the river's edge. A whispered word, a creak of timbers – and the boat shot away on the racing tide.

No alarm was raised that night. Why should it be? The appointed warder had done his rounds at the regulation time, checking that all was in order before locking the doors. He had approached the curtained bed, respectfully bade 'Goodnight, my Lord' and received a murmured, drowsy reply. He had then locked up securely and returned to his own quarters.

The warder's complacency was however due to be severely

74

The Bloody Tower archway

shaken. The next morning he returned, unlocked the door and entered – to stop, eyes wide with disbelief, for there, sitting up in bed was the servant wench, wearing Lambert's nightcap! 'In the name of God, Joan, what make you here? Where is my Lord Lambert?' he gasped. The girl shrugged her shoulders. 'He is gone, but I cannot tell whither!'

The consequences were of course predictable. Poor Joan was hauled before the Lieutenant of the Tower, then placed in custody. Search parties set off in pursuit, the City was combed by armed men, and a reward of £100 was offered. Lambert, one of the few men who could muster any real threat to the upsurge of Royalist reaction, had to be caught – and quickly.

The fugitive had travelled hard and secretly. Moving rapidly across country he made contact with other like-minded officers, old colleagues of his, and together they rode north to Edgehill in Warwickshire. There, on 22 March, their small force of six troops of horse was attacked by Colonel Ingoldsby and his men. Lambert's disheartened soldiers fled, and Lambert and his friends were placed under arrest.

Two who had rowed him to freedom also had been rounded up, for on 7 April Serjeant Northfolk, Serjeant at Arms, was instructed to hold Thomas Doyly and Alexander Taylor in Lambeth House prison, on suspicion of being privy to Lambert's escape.

Back in the Tower, John Lambert was put on trial. The monarchy had been restored, Charles II was now King, but leniency was shown. As the prisoner had played no part in the execution of Charles I, Lambert was banished to Castle Cornet, in Guernsey, a frowning fortress perched high on rocky cliffs. There he stayed from October 1661 until June the next year, when he was again tried, this time for high treason. At his trial he was discreet and submissive, perhaps hoping to win an easier prison. The verdict of guilty could have cost him his head, but again it was reduced to banishment – back to Castle Cornet, though he was now granted limited freedom within its bounds.

The man was incorrigible. In the Castle he appeared to settle down, exhibiting his talent for painting and gardening. For four years he lulled his guards into complacency and then, in 1666, his spirit unbroken, he attempted escape yet again!

But this time there was no wench to wear his nightcap, no strong oars to ferry him across the sea. He was caught, close confined, and watched night and day.

The final blow came in 1670. Under heavy escort he was transferred to St Nicholas's Fort, situated on a narrow strip of rock only three hundred yards long, called St Nicholas Isle, in Plymouth Sound. This lonely outpost, now known as Drake's Island, is less than a mile from the mainland, but for John Lambert it might well have been twenty times that distance. Now over fifty years of age, ten of them spent as a prisoner, his soul must have wearied. Roundhead dreams had melted like the sea mists that swirled around his desolate island prison, and even a successful escape would have been an empty victory, for whom could he have led?

His wife frequently brought some of their ten children to visit him and then, two days before Christmas 1676, sadly she died. Resigned to his lonely fate, he endured the harsh rigours of cold walls and bleak winds until on the 28 March 1684 he too passed away, after twenty-four years in prison. United at last, the Lamberts lie buried in St Andrew's Church in Plymouth, Devon.

All men aspire to make their mark on history, and John Lambert was no exception. His second daughter married Captain John Blackwell, a gentleman who was appointed

Governor of Pennsylvania in 1688 — just twenty years after William Penn, founder of that colony, was himself a prisoner in the Tower of London.

And as for our Colonel: brave as he was, and hard as he fought, let us remember how, as a prisoner tending his little garden in Castle Cornet, he cultivated a new species of flower, and so was known as 'The Knight of the Golden Tulip'.

9. Forde, Lord Grey:
Dashing Adventurer

'Tis one thing to be a love locked out,
And yet another for a prisoner
To be barred from entry!
All night must I sit tightly
Next the lesser gentry
In a tavern by the gate.
But wait!
This is a game that two can play.
Without a welcome,
Who am I to stay?

The conspirators' clock from the scene of the Ryehouse Plot, still in use in the Crown Tavern, Clerkenwell Green, London.

To 'lop' the King and his brother, that was the plot. And when Charles II and his heir James had been killed, why, that would be the end of the dissolute Court and its degenerate ways. Then we could have as a Protestant King, James, Duke of Monmouth.

Some of the conspirators, the noblemen and intellectuals, would have been content merely to exile the royal brothers. The others, maltsters and vintners, carpenters and cheesemongers, hotheads all, had more murderous intentions. Under their leaders, strangely enough an Englishman, an Irishman and a Scotsman, they planned to ambush the King and his brother as they returned from attending the races at Newmarket. An accomplice owned Rye House Farm, near Hoddesdon in Hertfordshire, on the royal route. There one member of the gang would block the road with a cart. Others would open fire from behind a wall, then the mounted party would charge and wipe out the royal troop.

But, then as now, rulers relied on efficient security services, and Charles was no exception. A drunken boast, a careless whisper in a tavern, and the plot was uncovered. A few confessed, names were named, and aristocrats and commoners alike were swept into the net.

One captured on that fateful summer day in 1683 was Forde, Lord Grey de Werke. A tall debonair figure, his good looks and dashing manner impressed the ladies considerably. Indeed his affair with his wife's attractive sister, daughter of the Earl of Berkeley, was the talk of the Court.

Now however his companion was a King's Messenger, one Henry Denham, bearer of a Royal Warrant for Lord Grey's arrest and committal to the Tower.

The two men arrived at the castle in the late evening. The gates were shut, the orders strict: no admittance. This was no real hardship, for two gentlemen could always while away the time over a few glasses of wine in one of the many taverns clustering around the Tower of London. Such ale houses were the haunt of the garrison soldiers, the warders and the watermen who plied for hire along the river, and although their company was rough and ready, at least the tavern was warm – and remained open all night.

The prisoner and his escort chatted and supped their wine, Denham relaxing in the presence of an obviously cultured gentleman, Lord Grey showing little or no concern about the outcome of his arrest. But behind his easy manner his thoughts raced. His generosity was having results, for Denham was now flushed and drowsy. However, even a sleeping escort would be of little advantage, for the area swarmed with off-duty soldiers, while their comrades, the sentries, patrolled outside the Bulwark Gate, mere yards from the tavern door. He would just have to bide his time and watch for the hint of a chance.

The night dragged on. Around him men slumped over the rough-hewn tables; others argued over their tankards. Some sang, but none loud enough to wake the gently inebriated Denham, who slept, head on folded arms. Lord Grey forced himself to be patient. He'd always relied on his quick wits, his ability to see, then seize, an opportunity, so he tried to rest while he could.

Byward Tower, with the Sally Port drawbridge on the right

Morning was heralded by the creak and clang of the Tower gates being swung open. Both men stirred, stretching and yawning, then stepped into the street. It was just after dawn. Lord Grey surveyed the scene with narrowed eyes. The sentries paced, guarding gateway and walls, preventing a quick dash for freedom. One cry, one shot, and the whole district would be alive with troops.

Almost languidly he followed his escort, pausing to exchange a few words with the sentry. Across to the Middle Tower he sauntered, commenting to the guard there how unjust it all was, but that a few words with his friend the Lieutenant, Captain Tom Cheek, would clear the matter up. Meanwhile his escort Denham, mission accomplished now that his prisoner had entered the Tower's confines, relaxed and strode on ahead, thinking only of a good wash followed by breakfast.

As Lord Grey approached the Byward archway he suddenly recalled the layout of that tower. Guardrooms lay each side within the thickness of the archway, and beyond the right-hand one was a side entrance leading out on to the wharf. This was the Sally Port, traditionally the royal entrance. Persons of note disembarked at the King's Steps and then, crossing the wharf, entered via the Sally Port, thus by-passing the gates and main drawbridges. It was always guarded.

He passed through the Byward archway, casually looking about him. Servants, workmen, were starting to arrive, to stop and chat; the castle was slowly beginning to wake up. Lord Grey nodded to one or two passers by, conscious that every slow step was taking him deeper and deeper into the State prison. And then his heart missed a beat – for the Sally Port guard was nowhere to be seen!

With a physical effort he forced himself to maintain his leisurely pace. Denham, his escort, was now well ahead, suspecting nothing. Hardly daring to breathe, Lord Grey turned right and, passing through the two ancient doorways, traversed the little drawbridge and emerged on to the wharf. His every sense alert for a sudden shout, a pounding of feet, he crossed to the King's Steps. There, as if in answer to a prayer, rocked a boat, its owner plying for hire! Within seconds he had boarded it, within hours he was down river at Greenwich; and within days he reached Holland, to join other supporters of the Duke of Monmouth.

The King's vengeance was swift. Henry Denham, King's Messenger, was severely punished, being committed to the Tower for six months, and Robert Lock, mariner, was thrown into Marshalsea Gaol accused of aiding Lord Grey, though he begged for mercy, having lost a leg in the King's service!

Lord Grey's adventures were however far from over. In 1685 James, Duke of Monmouth, landed in the West Country to raise an army, overthrow James II and take over the throne. In the campaign Lord Grey commanded the cavalry, fighting hard and well, but the Monmouth Rebellion failed completely and its leaders were captured. The Duke and Lord Grey were brought to Whitehall and there, at the house of Thomas Chaffinch, son of the erstwhile Keeper of the Jewels, they faced the King they had sought to overthrow. Monmouth pleaded for mercy, but was condemned to death for high treason. Lord Grey, it is said, admitted guilt but did not ask for forgiveness.

On 13 July 1685 they were taken to the Tower of London in the King's Barge, escorted by other barges filled with soldiers. Two nights and one day later James, Duke of Monmouth, suffered hideous death beneath the axe on Tower Hill.

Lord Grey remained in prison. It is reported that he seemed unconcerned despite the fate that awaited him, indeed he chatted and joked, even about Jack Ketch the executioner. Did

Forde, Lord Grey de Werke

he know that he would escape the axe even as he had escaped from the Tower? Some authorities believe that he turned King's informer, revealing fellow conspirators in the Rye House Plot, though the gossip of the day hinted at an affair between Monmouth and Grey's wife, with the jealous lord wreaking vengeance in betrayal.

Be that as it may, Lord Grey was pardoned on 12 November 1685 and 'restored in blood and estate'. In 1695 the Protestant King William III created him Earl of Tankerville, and he died in 1701.

Plotter or patriot, informer or dashing hero, he kept his nerve – and thus his head.

10. *Maguire and McMahon: Rebel Irish*

As I put hand to hand
A tiny closet is there formed
Within the circle of each palm,
And in it I may breathe
The secrets of my soul.

As I put hand to heart
My very being is thus warmed
And each and every harm
Is beat away, as birds take flight
Upon the bell's first toll.

As I put hand to mouth
In awe of all the glory that hath stormed
The strongest bastions of my doubt,
May I so slip away
Either to freedom or the scaffold's sway,
It matters not what cometh either way,
My faith is whole.

Even brave men have to suffer if the tides of fate are running against them, and so it was with Cornelius Maguire, 2nd Baron Enniskillen, and his friend Colonel Hugh Oge McMahon.

In the year 1641 England was otherwise engaged with Scotland, and so the time seemed ripe to raise Catholic Ireland. Devout men both, Lord Maguire was also deep in debt, and an uprising could well restore his fortunes. Colonel McMahon, who had seen service with the Spanish Army, recruited helpers for the first stage of the plot, the capture of Dublin Castle. One recruit was a servant of Sir John Clotworthy, a man named Owen O'Connolly who, though a Protestant, professed Catholic leanings.

The attack on the castle was planned for Saturday, 23 October 1641, and on the previous day O'Connolly met Colonel McMahon in that city. Whether O'Connolly was an informer, or just a man appalled by the prospect of the intended slaughter, is uncertain. Indeed his master, Sir John Clotworthy, boyhood friend of Lord Maguire, could also have been involved in the betrayal, for that gentleman re-enters our story in rather a surprising rôle.

Upon hearing McMahon's plan of attack, O'Connolly later eluded his vigilance and, seeking out the Lord Justices, revealed the entire conspiracy. Colonel McMahon resisted arrest but was brought before the Council, as was Lord Maguire.

Interrogation began, and McMahon, loyal to his Cause and his colleagues, proved stubborn. The Council loosened his tongue by loosening his joints; he was racked severely, and 'confessed enough to destroy himself and impeach some others'. Imprisoned, he was sent to the Tower after sentence of death had been passed upon him.

Lord Maguire, doubtless because of his title, was not racked but, being a dupe rather than a leader, admitted all the material facts. Late 1643 found the two men imprisoned in, some think, either the Martin or the Devereux Towers within the Tower of London, with an allowance of seven shillings per week each for food and kindling.

Both men, brave and determined, had come a long way together, and therefore resolved to get out together. Notes were passed to sympathizers in the city, money raised and, if hearts weren't softened, palms were greased. Two men, purporting to be priests from the Spanish Embassy, visited the prisoners (how useful were those voluminous cassocks?) and the plan was put into action.

One day in August 1644, as the sunlight streamed in through the arrow-slit to form a golden cross glowing on the opposite wall, the two men prepared for their escape. Among the food sent in that day to augment their meagre prison rations was a loaf, somewhat indigestible as, baked within it, was a note informing them of the location of a length of rope hidden on the outer wall battlements. And that evening, while one kept watch, the other used a saw previously smuggled in to cut through door hasps and bolts.

Stealthily they crept out in the darkness, then down the steps and into the outer ward. There, every sense aquiver, they moved from shadow to deeper shadow, hardly daring to breathe as noisy potboys and warders' children clattered past in the flickering torchlight, and sentries marched to take over duties from others. The two men sped across the open spaces and up on to the outer battlements above either Brass Mount or Legges Mount, both high gun positions on the northern wall. In the dark corner they found the rope; a few turns round a nearby stanchion, and they were quickly slithering down it into the murky waters of the moat. Both good swimmers, they were soon scrambling up the opposite bank, where their friends were waiting. They were free!

Alas, not for long. A reward of £100 encouraged the hue and cry, and on 19 September they were found in a house in Drury Lane by the Lieutenant of the Tower, Sir Isaac Pennington and, by an odd coincidence, a 'servant of Sir John Clotworthy'! Was that servant the informer O'Connolly? Did Sir John Clotworthy know of the hideout's existence beforehand? We shall never know, but the circumstances would seem to be as muddy as the waters of the moat. Incidentally, the reward did little for the erring Lieutenant, for he was fined £200 as a punishment for not preventing the escape.

Both Maguire and McMahon were close confined, strictly guarded in their cells. McMahon, found guilty of high treason, was hanged at Tyburn on 22 November 1644. Asked if any should pray for him, he replied curtly, 'None but Roman Catholics.'

Lord Maguire fought for time, for clemency. He claimed that, as an Irish peer, he should be tried in Ireland. He was over-ruled. He then claimed that as a baron he was entitled to death by the honourable axe rather than the ignoble rope. That also was rejected.

And on 20 February 1645 Cornelius Maguire endured the taunts and jeers of the crowd, and died bravely for his religion at Tyburn Tree, having forgiven all his enemies.

11. *Royalists and Jacobites*

E *ven as the sun sets*
S *o is it arisen*
C *ross the sea*
A *fter the manner of eternity.*
P *lace then thy trust*
E *ver steadfast*

I *n all things warranted,*

S *eeing white as white —*
H *alf-measures all dismissed —*
A *nd black as black,*
L *est the grey of the pigeon's wing*
L *eadeth thee aside from thy determination.*

Some names, such as Parliamentarians, Covenanters, Pilgrim Fathers, conjure up a sturdiness, a solid respectability that are essential qualities in our humdrum way of life. But equally essential are the names that set the imagination racing, not necessarily because they were *better* men, but because the very sound of the words implies a daredevil spirit which, were it not for our domestic commitments, we would willingly adopt! Names like the Crusaders, Merchant Adventurers, and the Knights Templar.

Two similar bands of men were the Royalists and the Jacobites, men who, fighting for lost causes, somehow produced the flair, the daring that we admire today.

So it is hardly surprising that among their ranks were men who could not, would not, sit meekly in the prisons of their captors and await their fate, but would strive mightily for freedom.

Men like Daniel O'Neile, a Royalist arrested for treason and sent to the Tower. In 1643 he escaped dressed as a woman, the guards mistaking him for a warder's wife. Fleeing to Brussels he later joined Charles II and fought for his King as a Lieutenant Colonel in the cavalry.

Four excellent examples of this calibre of men were the Royalist officers captured after the Battle of Worcester on 3

September 1651: Dalyell, Montgomery, Middleton and Massey.

Thomas Dalyell, forty-four years of age, and a General Major of Foot in the battle, was committed to the Tower on 16 September that year, 'five shillings per week allowed for his maintenance'. Eight months later he escaped, by methods unknown, and sailed to the Continent. In 1654 he raised a rebellion in Scotland and despite being wanted 'dead or alive', with a price of £200 on his head, he returned to France.

Doubtless bored by the lack of action there, he joined the Russian Army, Czar Alexis Michaelovitch promoting him Lieutenant-General. In between fighting the Tartars and the Turks, Dalyell introduced a more regular system of discipline into the Russian regiments. Later, as a full General, he rejoined Charles II, the Czar testifying that he was 'a man of virtue and honour, and of great experience in military affairs'. He became Commander-in-Chief in Charles' army, being known as the 'Muscovy General', and was renowned for his tough military ability, his eccentricity and appearance, for he wore a wide-brimmed beaver hat, no wig on his bald head, and swore never to shave following the execution of Charles I. He died suddenly of apoplexy in the summer of 1685, after a glorious, hectic and eventful life, thirty-three years after escaping from the Tower of London.

Major-General Robert Montgomery was another captive of the Roundheads, but not only did he escape from the Tower after three years' imprisonment, but following his recapture he was confined in Edinburgh Castle – and promptly escaped from there, too!

A fellow officer was Lieutenant-General John Middleton who, in his younger days, had a great friend, Laird Boccani. Together they made a pact that the first to die would reappear in spirit form to the other.

After the battle of Worcester, in which he was wounded, Middleton was 'prisoner in the Tower, under three lockes'. One night he awoke to find his friend Boccani by the bed. Middleton asked him if he were alive or dead, to which the answer came, 'Dead!'

The apparition, it is reported, then confirmed that he was indeed a ghost, and prophesied that within three days Middleton would escape. And without further ado 'the ghost gave a frisk and, saying

> "Givenni givanni, 'tis very strange,
> In the world to see so sudden a change",

it gathered up and vanished'.

With or without supernatural assistance, though doubtless encouraged by the prophecy, Middleton *did* escape, wearing his wife's clothes. He joined Charles II in France and, after the Restoration, was knighted for his services, taking the title of Earl of Middleton. These escapes by Royalists infuriated Oliver Cromwell, indicating as they did bribery or inefficient guarding. A reward of £200 was offered for Middleton's recapture; the warder responsible for his security was questioned and committed to Newgate Prison, and the maid involved was also confined there.

Middleton's colleague, Lieutenant-General Edward Massey, was also wounded but managed to escape in August 1652, though no details of his method exist. He hid in London for a few weeks, then joined the King in Paris, and was knighted in 1660.

A lucky man was Colonel Mallory, a Royalist caught plotting, in 1658, to overthrow the Roundhead Government. Somehow he got out of the Tower, was recaptured, and survived until Charles II was restored to the throne, when he was released.

Men who had an even more forlorn hope than the Royalists were the Jacobites. Plot and fight as they might, the Stuarts never regained the throne, and some of their most famous supporters were committed to the Tower. Most, alas, were executed, some escaped and prospered, and one got away but was caught and held in the Tower. He was Edward, Lord Griffin, imprisoned on 24 June 1690. Somehow he fled the Tower and after recapture was sentenced to death. However, Queen Anne reprieved him, and after twenty years in the Tower, he died in the winter of 1710. His name is inscribed on the brass tablet in the Chapel Royal of St Peter ad Vincula, the list which includes the executed Queens and others who similarly suffered.

1715 saw the first Jacobite uprising. It was quelled, and among those caught was Sir William Wyndham. No ordinary story, his, but one involving prophecy and an eerie fate! When he was a boy, a travelling fortune-teller visited his family home and spelt out the future for the servants of the household. As the fellow was deaf and dumb, he prophesied for William Wyndham by writing on the ground 'beware of the white horse'.

Years later Wyndham was touring abroad and happened across an Italian fortune-teller in Venice. To his utmost surprise,

The Middle Tower, bearing the arms of George I

the man also warned *'cavete il bianco cavallo!'* (beware the white horse).

After capture in 1715, Sir William Wyndham was brought to the Tower of London. In a carriage, and escorted by the Lieutenant, he approached the entrance. His arrival coincided with the workmen fixing an emblem over the archway of the Middle Tower. The emblem, which can still be seen there, was the coat of arms of George I, on whose orders Wyndham had been arrested – and the emblem included an heraldic white horse! Wyndham told his friends of this remarkable coincidence, though he must have thought that his luck had changed, for he escaped from his prison. However, his father-in-law, the Duke of Somerset, persuaded him to surrender himself, and after a year's further imprisonment he was released on bail.

Many years later while out hunting, his mount slipped and fell. He was thrown off and fatally injured, but doubtless could hardly have avoided it – for he was riding a white horse!

From horses to wigs, and here another Jacobite enters the arena. He was Donogh McCarthy, fourth Earl of Clancarty, who commanded a troop of horse, on the losing side, when the city of Cork fell to the forces of the Earl of Marlborough in 1690.

Stripped of his estates, Clancarty was sent to the Tower, but four years later, on 27 October 1694, his warder found, not the prisoner, but Clancarty's wig resting on its block, nestling on the pillow. With it was a note 'This block must answer for me!' He got away to France, though secretly visited his wife in London. Betrayed by a relative he was retaken, and although King William pardoned him, he was forced to live abroad.

First the Tower, then its French equivalent, the Bastille, were the 'homes' of Colonel John Parker, Jacobite. In 1693 he was involved in an assassination plot and the following year was committed to the Tower. His escape resulted in the Constable, Lord Lucas, being punished, and Colonel Parker fled to France. His career on the Continent must have been equally turbulent, for we learn that in 1702 he was locked up in the Bastille for insulting Mary of Modena.

The same uprising of 1715 swept many Scottish lords into prison: Nithsdale, Kenmure, Derwentwater and others. Examples had to be made, deterrents created, and so they were denied a trial, Parliament deciding their fate. Some were persuaded to plead guilty, being assured of leniency if they did; they were then sentenced to death! One, George Seton, fifth Earl of Wintoun, had a mind of his own and pleaded not guilty. Astutely he asked for time to assemble his defence. He was granted four days. Scotland and the north were under deep snow, communications at a standstill, and again Wintoun appealed for more time, because on points of law he was, as he said 'an ignorant man'.

He may not have known what to do at the bar of the court, but the bars of his prison could have told a different story! For as repeated petitions extended his stay of execution, so they provided time for his escape bid. He had obtained a file, and had bribed his warders not to visit him too often at night while he patiently worked away. To quote one historian 'he was busy with his pen during the day and his file during the night'.

And long after sentence had been carried out on his fellow officers, he broke out of his cell and got safely away to the Continent. It is believed that the whole affair was hushed up in view of the daring escape by his friend the Earl of Nithsdale earlier that year, although Wintoun's warder, Adam Mason, was severely punished. Wintoun was never recaptured and died in Rome thirty-three years later.

12. *Knights and Knaves*

A fig for sunshine!
I would have
The thickest fog
In manufacture
From the heavens,
Swirling and sniping
At my cloak,
And stealing
The raven's raucous croak
To render it a whisper.

As I have saved a penny gainst a rainy day,
And some sweet maid yet to be kiss't,
I would cast these fine treasures full away,
To flee this prison in a kindly mist.

Any prison in use for eight centuries 'entertains' within its walls a wide variety of prisoners, even one predominantly used to confine the king's personal enemies. Every known crime has at one time or another been represented at the Tower, from illegal duelling to killing a poacher, from 'quarrelling and ill language' to 'leading a life of dissipation'.

So it was a mixed gang indeed which broke out one day in 1422, Sir John Mortimer, Thomas Payne, John Cobham, Sir John Brakemond, Thomas Seggiswyk and Marcellinus from Genoa. Held on assorted charges, treason, heresy, being enemies of the State, it seems to have been a spontaneous attempt, the men perhaps being members of a working party on the outskirts of the Tower. All were caught except Seggiswyk; rewards were handed out to the captors, and William Yerd, Lieutenant of the Tower, received a years' imprisonment.

On many occasions the rewards to the successful searchers were well merited, as not all fugitives surrendered meekly. In 1378 two gentlemen, Hauley and Shakell, were accused of harbouring a prisoner of war. Somehow they got out of the Tower and sought sanctuary in Westminster Abbey, where they were immediately besieged by troops. Fighting broke out within those hallowed walls, and Hauley was killed. Shakell was returned to the Tower, but his subsequent penalty is not known.

Sometimes the records are but a single line, as for Sir John de

Molines, a prisoner of the Scottish wars in 1340. He escaped and was pardoned six years later. Other entries hint at rare adventures, each worth a book if only more were known; for instance Sir Humphrey Neville, who in 1461 plotted a revolt supporting King Henry VI. After getting out of the Tower, Neville was pardoned and even knighted, but that was not the end of the story, for in 1469 we find him joining a revolution in France. Alas for Sir Humphrey, he was eventually beheaded at York.

Churchmen, commoners, noblemen, given the opportunity, escaped. The Dean of Ely, chaplain to Archbishop Laud, spent six years in the Tower, leaving surreptitiously in 1648. Retaken, he was released two years later. And one can foresee the chance of escape when major disease ravages a city; William Lea, held for treason, did, and got away 'during the plague time of 1665'. Even noblemen with crazy ideas were taken seriously, especially by Queen Elizabeth's advisers, for in October 1561 Sir Anthony Fortescue was tried with others at Westminster Hall, for plotting an invasion by six thousand men from France in order to place Mary Queen of Scots on the throne. They had even engaged the services of two soothsayers, John Prestall and Edward Cosyn, who had conjured up a wicked demon, which promptly forecast Elizabeth's death within a year. All were spirited into the Tower (except the demon, it is hoped!) for long sentences, although Sir Anthony Fortescue had influence in high places and was allowed to escape.

At times magic jostled shoulders with sheer farce, as in the case of a Mr Short, who in 1629 was suspected of treason. He must have been the subject of many a bawdy quip, a ribald comment in the taverns of the day, for after sawing through bars and 'creeping out of a hole too narrow indeed for a cat', he lurked in the city posing as a Frenchman, and although his wife's house was under observation, he visited her frequently.

For some time he avoided recapture, though on one occasion he was 'forced to leave his breeches behind'. Such devotion, however, brought its penalty, for eventually he was caught and given a prison sentence.

Prisoners and warders alike could always rely on one thing. Both would be punished after an escape bid, but doubtless the risk — or the bribe, if any — was worth it. When John Tudor broke out in May 1654, both his warders, William Tasborough and John Gillet, lost their jobs and were gaoled in the Tower. Similarly a warder and two domestics finished up on the wrong side of the bars when William Arton got away in October 1673. Some prisoners suffered appallingly, though not necessarily because they had escaped. In 1413, Sir John Oldcastle, a gentle and kindly man, with other Lollards seeking to reform the Church's rôle in society, was charged with heresy. Friends helped him escape from the Tower but, later recaptured, he suffered the agonizing fate of being burned to death in St Giles's Fields.

Equally savage was the final sentence imposed on the handsome and reckless Sir Roger Mortimer who became the lover of Queen Isabella. They plotted the downfall of the King, Edward II, and Mortimer was sent to the Tower. There, after two years' scheming, he got away. During the celebrations on the Feast of St Peter ad Vincula he drugged his guards' wine, clambered up the wide kitchen chimney and scaled the walls using a rope ladder. With £1000 on his head he evaded capture until 1330, when he was caught in Nottingham Castle. Dragged back to the Tower of London, he was loaded with chains and secured in the deepest dungeon. Later, before a vast crowd at Tyburn Tree, he was hanged, drawn and quartered, his remains being left for display on the gibbet for six days, as an awful warning to all.

The White Tower, one of its upper windows providing a way of escape for Bishop Flambard.

But who was the first prisoner to escape? And who the last? The earliest recorded was Bishop Flambard, 'Ralf the Firebrand', minister, militant, taxgatherer and favourite of William Rufus, son of the Conqueror. But William died unexpectedly in 1100, and his successor Henry I imprisoned Flambard to placate the Londoners, who had long hated the Firebrand.

Flambard was no fool. Immensely rich, he surrounded himself in the White Tower with retinues of servants and lived like a lord, with nightly banquets for himself and the Norman knights guarding him.

And at Candlemas, February 1101, with his custodians lying befuddled around the hall, he opened his secretly marked wine jar and pulled out the rope it contained. His crozier under one arm, bags of gold under the other, he lowered himself from the uppermost window on the south side of the White Tower. A stout, heavy man, his hands were quickly cut to the bone by the rope, and a further hazard arose, for his calculations were wrong, and he had been sent a 45 foot rope for a 65 foot drop! Unable to climb back he fell heavily, but assistants were waiting to help him. In those early years the defences were minimal, and who should know the route better than Flambard – Constable of the Tower from 1098 to 1100!

He got away to Normandy but returned two years later, forgiven, to complete Durham Cathedral and to build Norham Castle on the river Tweed.

And the last prisoner to escape – so far? Well, in 1916, during the first World War, a young officer was confined in the Tower. No high treason, no assassination plot involved, just a little trouble concerning some cheques. A sentry stood outside his door, other officers visited him periodically to make sure everything was in order, and the young officer got bored and thought wistfully of his club in the West End. So after a couple of visitors had left him, and a new sentry taken post, he put on his hat and walked out.

Soldiers saluted him, as did the policeman at the front gate. He strolled to the nearest Underground Station and was whisked off to the bright lights. After a convivial evening and a pleasant breakfast, he realized the error of his ways, and so caught the Tube back again. Acknowledging the salutes, he returned to his Tower quarters, to learn of the alarm and search currently being conducted throughout London.

Doubtless the senior officers at his court martial understood, and even sympathized with his youthful escapade, for he received only a minor punishment.

So covering an incredible span of over eight hundred years, from Flambard in 1101 to a young Army Officer in 1916, prisoners attempted escape – and we applaud those few who succeeded.

13. *The Lady has the Last Word!*

Let the devil deliver the worst he can dole,
I shall charm him, disarm him and softly cajole,
Till never the twain shall ye tell us apart,
What with me and my wiles and his eboned old heart.

I will dance him along from my cell to the moat.
From the wharf to the river and into a boat,
Till his tail is a-flutter like some banderole,
And his eyn shineth bright as a sly forest stoat.

Oh, such are the gifts God to woman hath given,
For to lead sin awry she shall surely be shriven!

Charge your glasses for I give you a toast; to Alice Tankerville, the only woman prisoner to escape from the Tower of London. Her story involves the highest and the lowest, from Parliament to a common servant; theft, suffering, daring and devotion are the classic ingredients with, alas, an unhappy ending.

In 1531 Parliament was gravely concerned over the theft of 366 French crowns while in transit by sea. These gold coins, 'which every man in Cologne says have been stolen', were a veritable fortune in those days, and the finger of accusation pointed at one John Wolf. He was brought to the Tower of London in 1533 and while there, Mistress Wolf his wife, though known as Alice Tankerville, visited him frequently. During these visits she made the acquaintance of two of the Lieutenant's servants, William Denys and John Bawde, men who were to play a vital part in her life.

Her husband was released, probably because of lack of evidence, and went to Ireland, but before he left he asked John Bawde to befriend his wife whilst he was away.

It would seem that events now moved quickly, implicating Wolf and Alice in the robbery, for they were attainted by Parliament. That is, the case was heard, discussed and tried by the Members without a legal trial in Court or indeed the presence of the accused at any hearing. Man and wife were sentenced to death, and Alice Tankerville, heavy iron shackles on wrists and

110

ankles, was imprisoned in Cold Harbour Tower within the Tower of London.

Cold Harbour, now demolished, was a twin drum bastion adjoining the west side of the White Tower, and Alice was confined in an inner room. So harsh were her conditions that the Lieutenant's daughter interceded on her behalf. Eventually some mercy was shown and the irons were struck from her limbs.

William Denys, the servant of the Lieutenant, now renewed his friendship with the lonely captive, visiting her so often that it came to the notice of the Lieutenant himself. Such unseemly conduct by his staff was not to be countenanced. William Denys was dismissed forthwith.

However, Alice was not neglected. Doubtless an attractive and good-natured girl, she was soon talking to her other friend John Bawde through the grating of her cell. To him she confided that Denys had revealed a secret route out of the Tower, and she beseeched Bawde to help her get away, to escape the death sentence that awaited her. Whether Bawde was spurred on by friendship, loyalty or affection for the girl, we will never know. But he bought two ropes for 13 pence from Sampson's house, and that night passed them to her through the grating for safe keeping. Such items in the servants' quarters of the Lieutenant's Lodgings would have caused commotion indeed.

The next morning he returned to Cold Harbour. There he revealed the details of the escape he had planned for them both, and collected the ropes. He also gave Alice a key which he had filed to fit the outer door of her prison, for John Bawde was nothing if not thorough.

At ten o'clock that night, after her warder's last rounds, Alice went into action. Lying on the floor of her cell she forced her

The Bloody Tower archway; its shadows doubtless concealed Alice
Tankerville as she fled via Traitors' Gate beyond.

arm beneath the ill fitting inner door, a long stick held in her hand. On her back, looking up blindly into the darkness, she probed on the other side of the door with the stick until she encountered the bone which held the hasp in position. While prodding with one hand, she shook the door with the other until suddenly the door swung open, almost hitting her. Scrambling to her feet she put the skeleton key to the outer door, and was away.

Through the shadows, cloak hood over her head, she glided through the archways and up the steps on to the flat roof of St Thomas's Tower. This tower, above Traitor's Gate, offered the best chance of escape, for the moat at that point was at its narrowest, only a few yards wide. There John Bawde awaited her, one end of the rope secured to an iron hook. Down the rope they slithered, swinging wide to land safely on the wharf. Bawde found a small boat there and together they drifted stealthily past the little houses clustered along the wharf to the east.

At the Iron Gate Steps they left the boat, for at the north-east side of the castle in the St Katherine area by Little Tower Hill, they would find two horses waiting. Thence they would ride to the house of Jeffrey Haryson, a friend who would hide them until the coast was clear. So with the moat to their left and mean huddled dwellings on their right, they walked up the lane. They could now relax after the tension and stress of the successful escape. After all, there was nothing suspicious about a couple walking along hand in hand, and the sensation of freedom must have been intoxicating to them both.

And then, as if in a nightmare, their luck suddenly and disastrously ran out. In the distance they saw lights as men approached. For one heart-stopping moment John and Alice must have feared the worst, but as the men neared them the couple relaxed again, for it was only the night-watch on patrol, their lanterns held high. Perhaps a greeting was exchanged, but a greeting that changed to a challenge – for a watchman named Gore knew, and recognized, Alice. It was the end.

Both were arrested and Bawde locked up temporarily in the Counter Gaol. He confessed everything and pleaded that he had been motivated 'only by the love and affection he bore to her'.

A letter among the State Papers of Lord Lisle, dated 28 March 1534, states

'Wolf and his wife Alice Tankerville will be hanged in chains at low water mark upon the Thames on Tuesday. John Bawde is in Little Ease cell in the White Tower dungeon, and is to be racked and hanged.'

May they rest in peace.

Select Bibliography

Her Majesty's Tower	Hepworth Dixon	1885
Memoirs of the Tower of London	Britton and Brayley	1830
History of the Tower	J. Bayley	1830
Tower of London from Within	G. Younghusband	1919
Tower of London	Morley and Stead	1903
General Williamson's Diary	C. Fox	1912
Tower of London Records		
Dictionary of National Biography		
The Penny Magazine		1836
Letters and Papers of the Reign of Henry VIII	Gairdner	1883